The
Practical
Coach

Anthony Connolly

ISBN: 1499552548
ISBN 13: 9781499552546

For Tara

My blessing

TABLE OF CONTENTS

PART IV: CONCLUSION

COACHING
IN THE REAL WORLD

The days were starting to run together for Laura. Up early to feed and walk the dog, then grab a cup of coffee and settle in for the 90-minute commute to the office. The long day at the office was followed by the commute home and the process repeated itself five days a week. The only good thing about the commute was that it gave her the chance to think about her team and why she wasn't making her revenue objective. Given how her team's results were trending, she needed to quickly ramp up her numbers. Meetings with her boss, Allison, were getting more uncomfortable. She wouldn't admit it to Allison but Laura knew she wasn't a superstar, but she had always been a solid performer and took pride in meeting her revenue objective.

Laura thought about the recent impacts to her team: a re-organization of the sales teams, the introduction of a new account management system, a big push on a couple of new products, and a recent price change by her biggest competitor. All had taken the steam out of her sales momentum.

Due to the recent re-organization, she was saddled with a couple of low performers (Jack and Francis) who weren't getting it done. She did have a couple of strong performers who always came through with little or no support from her, with emphasis on the "no". She had another five solid performers who were more hit than miss, and she could generally count on them to make their numbers.

She had also been assigned two new hires; Harvey and Tracey. Laura had to admit they seemed to have potential. Harvey was fresh out of college and had tested off the charts during the application process. Tracey was joining the team from the biggest competitor so Laura expected her to quickly get up to speed and provide some insight on the rationale for their recent price change.

Unfortunately, Harvey and Tracey were carrying a revenue objective equivalent to 50% of a full-time sales manager even though they were in new hire training about 75% of their time. Laura wondered how corporate headquarters set quotas. How can new sales managers sell anything if they are in training most of the day? If there was a silver lining to this cloud, she had two months before Harvey and Tracey would carry a full revenue objective.

As she merged onto the highway, she began to think about the coaching she needed to do for her team. If she focused on the new team members, who was going to figure out why Jack wasn't meeting his revenue target? He was making enough cold calls, and a good source told her he had gone back over the sales training program a second time after work. It appeared he was motivated, but he didn't seem to be gaining any traction in his sales.

As for Francis, if you showed her a spreadsheet, she could make it sing and dance. She had no problem getting existing customers to understand the economic value of continuing to do business with her, but she couldn't identify and develop new customer relationships. If Francis didn't start closing some new deals this month, Laura was going to have to "talk" with her.

Laura didn't like having the "talk"; the "do you really want to be here and if you do, you need to close some sales…." The "talk" always created drama in the office and the funny thing was, you couldn't predict the impact of the "talk". Some individuals tried harder for a while, and Laura suspected that was because they were looking for another job. Then they would give up or quit. A few individuals closed some new sales but you never knew how or if this new found ability would last. Most individuals argued with you about how unfair the process was and quit. It was nerve-wracking not knowing how things were going to turn out.

As she thought about the insanity of finding enough time to coach all eleven of her team members, she figured she'd use the old "fire" method of coaching that she had picked up informally over time. It was a simple approach: She'd look over her team's results for the previous day and the individual with the worst results became the designated "fire". She'd find time to coach the individual to put out the "fire". The next day, she'd do the same thing and the cycle would continue. Though she was sure it wasn't the best coaching process around, it was the only one she knew. At least she felt some sense of accomplishment when she identified a problem and made some effort to fix it even if results didn't necessarily improve over time.

She spotted her building coming up on the left and told herself she was going to spend the first 30 minutes of the day looking over yesterday's results. She'd then schedule one hour later in the day to coach the person with the worst results. She felt some sense of relief realizing that she had committed to do some coaching.

As she pulled into the parking lot and got out of her car, she heard the unmistakable long high whine of a fire alarm coming from inside the building. As she approached the front door, people started streaming out of the building, heading to their designated places in the parking lot. It was then she saw the sign, "Fire Alarm Drill Today", and laughed at the irony.

As she headed back to her designated place in the parking lot, she let out a long sigh. She knew she needed to be a more effective and efficient coach, but she didn't know how to do it and she was confident that even if she knew what to do, she wouldn't have the time to do it. What she needed was a simple and effective model that allowed her to focus her limited time on coaching efforts that made a difference.

She found her place in the parking lot. No coaching today, she thought to herself as she looked for her team members.

OVERVIEW

If Laura's story describes your experience with coaching, I can guarantee two things: You're not alone and this book can help you.

The Practical Coach is for anyone involved in coaching who believes in the value of simple and effective solutions. Within this book, you will find my coaching framework known by the acronym MOST™. MOST stands for the four phases of the coaching framework:

Phase 1: **Map** key skill gaps.
Phase 2: **Order** the resources that close key skill gaps.
Phase 3: **Structure** a coaching plan.
Phase 4: **Track** results.

We have the best of intentions when it comes to developing our team members' skills, but the reality is that the demands of our everyday jobs and personal lives make it difficult to find the time to create an effective coaching plan and put that plan into practice. The benefit of the MOST coaching framework is that it focuses on the key skills that drive performance improvement and results. This simple but effective approach ensures you don't waste time and effort coaching individuals who don't need coaching or coaching individuals in areas lacking an impact on results.

No special skill or talent is required to provide coaching that impacts results. You need to be motivated to coach, and you need a coaching framework. Achieving individual and team performance goals, driving organizational efficiency, improving your business acumen, building your reputation as a leader and obtaining a sense of accomplishment are all outcomes that best serve as motivation to coach. Using MOST as your coaching framework allows you to achieve these outcomes within the constraints of the real world in which you live and work.

In the following chapters, you'll find everything you need to know about how to use MOST to be a practical coach. The book begins with a discussion of the fundamentals of coaching and moves to a description, complete with working examples, of each of the four phases of MOST. The closing chapters discuss how best to implement MOST in your organization, provide a summary of key takeaways and conclude with a resolution of the coaching issues faced by Laura.

I've done six things to help make this book user-friendly:

1. I have invented three individuals to use as a reference when I am describing coaching

situations. You've met Laura, and I'll intro-
duce George and Jennifer in later chapters as
I work through coaching examples using the
MOST framework.

2. I've included an exercise at the end of each
   chapter that focuses on the key takeaways in
   that chapter. Answers to these exercises begin
   on page 133.

3. I have highlighted key points or themes with a
   gray background for easy reference.

4. From a punctuation standpoint, I use **bold**
   type any time I reference any of the four key
   phases of MOST and I use an underline to
   separate key sections of each chapter.

5. I've added a blank "Notes" page at the end
   of the book that you can use to jot down your
   own thoughts and ideas.

6. I've made the book small so it's easy to carry
   and reference as needed.

I wish you all the best with your coaching.

Chapter One:

WHAT IS COACHING?

I define coaching as a series of interactions between individuals focused on the identification and subsequent improvement of a key skill (or skills) needed to achieve an agreed-upon goal.

That sounds like a mouthful of corporate-speak so I will break it down and focus on the intent behind the definition.

<u>What is coaching?</u>

Coaching is a series of interactions. It is a two-way street involving not only dialogue between individuals but also activities performed by the coach and coachee. Anyone can initiate a coaching relationship. What is necessary is for both individuals to agree to have a coaching relationship. Though failure to meet a performance goal, such as achieving a sales target, can drive some type of mandated coaching relationship with the boss, engaging in a coaching relationship is not limited to boss/employee relationships.

Coaching is about the identification of the skills that drive performance. As a practical matter, skill refers to any defined capability such as the ability to create financial management models or communicate effectively.

Coaching is about improvement. Once you have identified the specific skill or skills linked to driving performance, you have to baseline the current skill level and determine how much these skill levels need to improve to achieve your goal. If you don't measure improvement, then coaching is a waste of time.

Coaching is about agreement. Most importantly, you need to agree upon the specific goals to achieve. Without agreement, you do not have coaching; instead, you have a one-way relationship where you use management techniques, such as directives and requirements, to drive performance.

<u>What coaching is not.</u>

Coaching is often confused with other activities that, though valuable in and of themselves, are not coaching. Three activities most often confused with coaching are training, mentoring, and managing. My perspective of these three activities is as follows:

1. Training

Training can be an effective component of coaching; you will want to look at all activities that can help the coachee build and reinforce a specific skill or skill set. Training involves activities such as taking classes, listening to presentations, attending conferences, or reading specific books.

What is often missing, however, is the relevance of the training to the improvement of the skill needed to achieve the agreed-upon definition of success. How will the training address a specific gap in the skill set? How do you measure the impact of training?

Without relevance, training often loses its impact, if it had any at all, soon after the individual leaves the training environment.

2. Mentoring

Mentoring involves career management discussions held with an individual's key contacts inside and outside their organization or company.

Mentoring can be either formal (a relationship the organization sets up) or informal (the individual independently seeking and finding a mentor). In either case, the mentor is willing to invest time and energy to provide guidance on a range of issues, such as organizational politics, insight into future opportunities and career management. The mentor potentially provides the organizational exposure needed to advance the mentee's career. Mentoring relationships with individuals outside the company can provide insight into the competitive landscape and a wider range of career opportunities. Whether a mentor is inside or outside your organization or company, a mentor should be respected and trustworthy and should be willing to listen to and speak the truth.

Mentors, however, may not have sufficient insight into the mentee's performance to provide meaningful feedback on their performance and or how to improve it. Additionally, mentoring may not be able to help the individual identify or build the specific job skills needed to succeed in the next opportunity the individual is considering.

3.   Managing

Managing is usually comprised of scheduled one-on-one discussions between an individual and their boss. During these discussions, the individual presents recent accomplishments, provides a status on existing issues, sets out a plan to address any areas of concerns, and discusses up-coming activities.

This feedback process is important but a discussion of whether your team member achieved their sales goals at the end of a particular sales cycle will not identify whether he or she has the communication skills needed to make an effective sales call or prospect for new leads.

My belief and the book's premise are that people who want to coach lack a simple and effective framework to coach. Due to this lack of a framework, it is easy to fall into the habit of using training, mentoring, or managing (or a combination of all three) as coaching.

This brings me back to my coaching framework known by the acronym MOST™. As I outlined in the Overview, the MOST framework has four phases:

Phase 1: **Map** key skill gaps.
Phase 2: **Order** the resources that close key skill gaps.
Phase 3: **Structure** a coaching plan.
Phase 4: **Track** results.

The benefit of the MOST coaching framework is that it focuses on the key skills that drive performance improvement and results. This simple but effective approach ensures you don't waste time and effort coaching individuals who don't need coaching or coaching individuals in areas lacking an impact on results.

Starting in Chapter Four, I will provide details of each phase of the MOST coaching framework.

Key takeaways

1. Coaching is a series of _____ between individuals focused on the _____ and subsequent _____ of a key skill needed to achieve an _____ goal.
2. Coaching is often confused with other activities such as _____, _____, and _____.
3. The MOST coaching framework simplifies the coaching process into _____ phases.

The answers are on page 133.

Chapter Two:

WHY COACH?

Before I take on most tasks, I do some level of cost/benefit analysis. The analysis can be as simple as determining how many holes of golf I could play if I did not spend time cleaning my garage on Saturday versus how unhappy my wife, Tara, will be if I don't clean the garage. However, when it comes to business decisions, a cost/benefit analysis can be complex given the high cost of making the wrong decision. This complexity results in a great deal of research into the cost/benefit models associated with certain business decisions.

Coaching is not, nor should it be, immune to this type of analysis. After all, coaching takes time and effort on your part and on the part of the individual you are coaching, and it consumes organizational resources. So, before we go into any detail about a coaching framework, let's talk about the benefits associated with coaching for the organization, the person being coached, and most importantly, for you.

I'll only touch briefly on the benefits for the organization and the person being coached because the focus of this book is you.

Organizational benefits of coaching

For organizations that support coaching, the well-documented benefits include the following six items:

1. Improved communications
2. Decreased levels of stress and tension
3. Enhanced employee satisfaction
4. Reduced employee turnover
5. Increased productivity
6. Increased customer satisfaction

In summary, a coaching culture directly and positively affects the organization's morale and bottom line.

Benefits for the individual you are coaching

Many of the benefits for the coachee are also well documented and overlap with those for the organization and include:

1. Decreased stress and tension
2. Improved satisfaction with the job and the organization
3. Skill development
4. Skill diversification
5. Potential for increased compensation
6. Increased influence over career opportunities

In summary, a coaching culture directly and positively affects the individual's morale and bottom line.

Benefits for the coach

As I stated in Chapter One, this book focuses on making you a practical coach by providing you with a simple and effective tool to drive individual performance through the identification and development of key job skills. To that end, this section of the chapter will focus on the benefits of using the MOST™ coaching framework as part of your approach to driving performance improvement, leading your organization and managing your career. The five key benefits of using MOST are the following:

1. Achievement of performance goals
2. Improvement of organizational efficiency
3. Improvement of business acumen
4. Reputation building
5. Sense of accomplishment

1. Achievement of performance goals

The key objective of any organization is to meet its performance goals. Whether the goal is a sales target, meeting budget, or completing a project on schedule, the organization's efforts must focus on the achievement of the goal(s). If you can define your goals, the MOST coaching framework provides a mechanism to improve performance and achieve those goals.

2.   Improvement of organizational efficiency

The MOST coaching framework is exactly that: a framework. This means three things:

a.   MOST doesn't lock you into a rigid set of processes for all individuals in your organization,
b.   MOST can be used with any employee, high potential or otherwise.
c.   MOST is a repeatable process.

When you use the first phase of MOST to **Map** the key skill gaps of the individual you are coaching, you may learn that certain individuals in your organization do not need coaching. You may find you can improve organizational performance by either moving individuals into different jobs that best match their skill sets, or changing some roles and responsibilities within existing jobs. In the cases where individuals do require coaching, MOST allows for the creation of a coaching plan that's detailed and tailored to the individual and his or her development of specific key skills. Because MOST is a focused approach to coaching, you and the individual you are coaching only spend time and effort on activities that directly impact results.

Within some organizations, the coaching tools available depend on whether you're coaching a high potential employee or a problem employee. High potential employees can be offered a Career Counseling Plan (CCP) focused on preparing them for promotion whereas the problem employee can be placed on a Development Plan (DP). The connotation here is that a DP is the last step in the Human Resources (HR) process to create the documentation needed to have the employee removed from the payroll. With MOST, no such connotation exists. MOST can be used with any employee, high potential or otherwise.

Lastly, when you use MOST to achieve a goal, you have a repeatable process. Your performance improvement is not a result of luck. You don't have to worry if lightning will strike twice. You simply follow the MOST framework.

3.   Improvement of business acumen

The **Structure** phase of MOST requires the creation of a coaching plan to improve the skills that link to the performance metrics and goals of your business. This phase requires a fundamental understanding of how your business operates, including why you created and selected specific performance metrics and goals. You need this understanding, and you need to be able to articulate this understanding, because you're going to hold yourself and others accountable to the achievement of the metrics and goals.

By working through the **Structure** phase of MOST, you will develop a deeper understanding of the fundamental relationships among you, your team's efforts, and your organization's bottom line. You will also develop the capacity to articulate these fundamental relationships.

4.   Reputation building

As stated earlier, by using the MOST coaching framework, individuals in your organization are going to develop new skills and enhance existing skills that lead to superior individual and team performance.

Performance improvement resulting from using the MOST coaching framework will also generate an important additional dividend: your reputation. You become known as someone who gets results through the focused development of your team members' skills, not employee intimidation or luck.

Your enhanced reputation will allow you to do the following:

a.   Attract, develop, retain, and seed talent in other organizations

i. People want to work and stay in success-ful organizations.

ii. People want to work and stay in organiza-tions that develop their skills.

iii. As you develop the skills of the individu-als on your team, some of them may look for opportunities outside your organiza-tion. You can leverage your reputation to influence where these individuals go to ensure their continued success.

b. Obtain needed resources

i. When you seek resources or assistance from other departments for your coaching efforts, you will have the credibility to ensure your requests are heard. Obtaining resources in any organization is difficult, but if you have developed a reputation such that people know their time, money, or effort will be valued, you will increase the chances of obtaining the needed re-sources.

c. Create a self-coaching and peer-to-peer coaching organization

i. As your team members become famil-iar with the MOST coaching framework and its benefits, you may see behaviors such as self-coaching and peer-to-peer coaching. Team members use the MOST coaching framework to work on their own skill set gaps (self-coaching) or look to work with their team members on their skill set gaps (peer-to-peer coaching). Achievement of self-coaching and peer-to-peer coaching is the summit of a high-performing and well-coached team; it doesn't happen often, but it is powerful to see in practice.

5.   Sense of accomplishment

This benefit may seem more theoretical than tangible but I believe it is no less important. Realizing our own potential and helping others realize their potential through coaching positively influences our self-esteem and sense of accomplishment.

An additional advantage of all of the above benefits is that they are self-perpetuating. The more you develop the talent on your team, the better your results. The better your results, the more your reputation will grow. The more your reputation grows, the more you will be able to attract, develop, retain, and seed talent, and the cycle will continue.

Key takeaways

1. A coaching culture directly and positively af-
    fects the organization's _____ line.
2. MOST is a _____ process.
3. Using MOST leads to:
    a. Achievement of _____ goals
    b. Improvement of organizational _____
    c. Improvement of business _____
    d. _____ building
    e. Sense of _____

The answers begin on page 133.

Chapter Three:

GUIDING PRINCIPLES

There are three guiding principles that define the MOST™ coaching framework. These principles originate from my more than 25 years of coaching and seeing the success that comes from creating coaching relationships based upon mutual respect, setting goals and ensuring ownership of the coaching plan. These principles apply to both the coach and coachee.

Simply put, the three guiding principles are the following:

1. Be respectful
2. Set goals
3. Take ownership

1.   Be respectful

You need to base your coaching relationship with an individual on respect. That respect begins with an understanding that the individual you are coaching is always aware of their success or lack of success. What the individual may not know is why they are successful or unsuccessful and by extension where or how to focus their efforts to improve performance and achieve the desired or required goal.

Using the MOST coaching framework to have an open and honest dialogue with the individual you are coaching on their key skills, gaps in those skills, and ways to close those gaps, makes the individual a partner in the coaching relationship. By doing so, you increase the opportunities to earn their trust and respect because you frame the coaching relationship as just that: a relationship.

2. Set goals

You must coach to a definable and measurable goal or set of goals. If you can't define and measure what you want to achieve, particularly when it comes to linking your coaching plan to performance objectives, you don't have a coaching plan. What you have, in that case, is a checklist of activities where completing the activity is success. Though value may exist in completing activities, in today's work environment you're not effectively utilizing your resources if you can't link activity to output and output to impact on key business goals.

3.   Take ownership

You as the coach have the responsibility to provide a coaching framework and environment that provides the person you are coaching the opportunity to be successful. However, when we speak of the execution of the coaching plan, the person you are coaching owns the plan. He or she must put in the effort needed to achieve the plan's goals. No coaching framework can make up for an individual's lack of ownership of the plan.

Key takeaways

1.   _____: Frame the coaching relationship as just that - a relationship.
2.   _____: Coach to a definable and measurable goal or set of goals.
3.   _____: The person you are coaching owns the coaching plan.

The answers are on page 134.

Chapter Four:

MAP

The four-step MOST™ framework provides the guidance to create a simple, yet effective coaching plan that drives performance improvement and results. As I outlined in Chapter One, the MOST framework has four phases:

Phase 1: **Map** key skill gaps.
Phase 2: **Order** the resources that close key skill gaps.
Phase 3: **Structure** a coaching plan.
Phase 4: **Track** results.

Throughout this chapter and the following chapters, I will work with George, in his Project Management (PM) role, to create a coaching plan. I have also included, in Chapter Ten, an additional coaching plan centered on Jennifer, a Sales Manager.

In this chapter, we're going to focus on the **Map** phase of MOST. This phase is comprised of three specific steps used to determine the key skills and the associated skill proficiency gap (if any) between the skills required by the job and the skills possessed by the individual.

<u>Phase 1: **Map**</u>

Map key skill gaps.

Step 1: Determine and list the job's key skills and required proficiency level.
Step 2: Determine and list the individual's key skills and proficiency level.
Step 3: **Map** the two lists to determine an inventory of key skill gaps.

To provide clarity, I will describe all three steps and illustrate all three steps with an example at the end of the chapter.

Step 1: Determine and list the job's key skills and required proficiency level.

Let's begin with my choice of the word skill. As a practical matter, skill refers to any defined capability. In many companies, each position has a defined list of the required and desired skills, experiences and educational requirements along with a description noting the activities associated with the position.

The difference between activities and skills is vitally important. For example, George, our PM, may have no reservations about setting up and running meetings for a project, but he lacks the communication skills to be effective in those meetings. In this case, the activity is running meetings but the skill is effective communications.

If you're faced with a situation where you don't know, or are unable to define, the key skills and their proficiency level required to be successful in the job, a number of options are available to you to answer this question. The following six options do not represent all options nor are they listed in any particular order; any action that gets you the information you need is fine:

1. Speak to individuals who have achieved success in similar jobs.
2. Review the job description from your HR group, if available.
3. Look at your own position and its required skills.
4. Speak to your peers and your boss.
5. Speak to clients and customers (if appropriate).
6. Think about other jobs you've had that have the same type of deliverables.

I recommend assessing the key skills required by the job before you inventory the key skills of the individual you're going to coach. By completing activities in this order, you can eliminate or reduce any positive or negative bias toward that individual. What I mean is if the individual is proficient in a certain area, you may be tempted to include that skill in the list of required job skills even if that skill is unrelated to achieving success. George, for example, may have in-depth computer programming skills, but if writing code is not critical to the success of his PM position, it shouldn't be on the list of job required skills.

As you create the list of skills required by the job, you will rate each of these skills on its required level of proficiency using a ten-point scale. With this scale, one (1) corresponds to a novice skill level, five (5) corresponds to an intermediate skill level, and ten (10) corresponds to an expert skill level. Do not spend a lot of time worrying about the difference between a five (5) and six (6) when assigning your ratings. You're looking to be directionally correct.

You're not rating the importance of each of the required skills relative to each other. The job requires each of the skills you list. What you're doing is independently rating the required proficiency level for each skill.

Step 2: Determine and list the individual's key skills and proficiency level.

We need to determine the individual's current skills and proficiency level of those skills. The following four options do not represent all options available to obtain the necessary information nor are they listed in any particular order; any option that gets you the information you need is fine:

1. Sit down with the individual and discuss his or her skills.
2. Look at the individual's overall body of work, including historical evaluations.
3. Speak with the individual's previous supervisor or skip-level supervisor.
4. Talk with the individual's internal and external clients or customers.

Discussions with previous supervisors, internal and external clients, or customers may not be possible or appropriate. In cases where you can have these discussions, however, you should focus on specific examples of the key skills the individual demonstrated to achieve the defined results. This approach also holds true when you speak with the individual you are going to coach. You're looking for specific examples of their use of their key skills.

I have often found that individuals can recite a long list of their work accomplishments and, in some cases, the specific results achieved, but they have little insight on the associated skills that achieved the results. For example, George may tell you that he is a good PM and when you ask him what makes him a good PM, he may say, "I've managed ten projects at a time", "people like working for me", or "my last five projects came in on time and under budget". You may even hear the familiar "I'm a people person." However, when you ask George to list the skills that make him a good PM, the answers may not come as quickly.

The creation of this list of skills and proficiency levels can be one of the most eye-opening activities of the coaching process. People are generally familiar talking about results they have achieved. What they are generally unfamiliar talking about are the skills needed to achieve their results. As you work through this process, it becomes one of discovery. People begin to recognize the skills they possess, and they become aware of what skills they need to possess to be successful.

As you and the individual work through compiling a list of their skills, you will need to rate those skills using the same one-to-ten scale used in Step 1.

Step 3: **Map** the two lists to determine an inventory of key skill gaps.

At this point, you have two lists; the list of skills and the associated proficiency levels required to achieve job success and the list of skills and the associated proficiency levels possessed by the individual.

This final step of the **Map** phase of MOST will allow you and the individual to identify where to focus your coaching efforts to have the greatest impact on results. The process associated with this final step of the **Map** phase is simple; **Map** the two lists to determine the skill proficiency gap (if any) between the skills required by the job and the skills possessed by the individual.

Now that we have a framework for the activities associated with the **Map** phase, I will work through an example using George in his PM role.

<u>George</u>
<u>PM Role</u>

<u>Phase 1: **Map**</u>

Step 1: Determine and list the job's key skills and required proficiency level.

You will create the list of key skills associated with the job, and rate the proficiency required for each of these skills using a ten-point scale where one (1) is novice and ten (10) is expert. Remember, you're not rating the importance of each of the skills relative to each other. The job requires each of the skills you list. What you're doing is independently rating the required proficiency level for each skill.

Your list of the key PM skills and their associated proficiency level needed to achieve success in that role is as follows:

Job Required Key Skill	Rating (1–10)
Communications (written and verbal)	10
Financial acumen (knowledge of operational impacts on financials)	8
PM software proficiency	7
Prioritization	7
Negotiation	7

Step 2: Determine and list George's key skills and proficiency level.

Your discussions with George must focus on skills, not activities. Let's assume that George talks about his following work experiences:

1. The rollout of a new software package
2. The selection of research and development projects that will be funded
3. The selection of the next country for expansion of the workforce
4. Marketing activities for a new product

What key skills were identified in this discussion?:

1. The rollout of a new software package
   a. Communications (bridging discussions between technical and non-technical personnel)
   b. Financial acumen (determining revenue forecasts/modeling sales)
   c. Prioritization (determining order of activities to meet launch date)

2. The selection of research and development projects that will be funded
   a. Technical expertise (understanding technology benefits)
   b. Financial acumen (understanding business case financials)
   c. Negotiation (getting agreement on priorities for the projects)

3. The selection of the next country for expansion of the workforce

    a.   Financial acumen (understanding business case financials)

    b.   Prioritization (determining impact on company image of having products made or supported offshore)

    c.   Negotiation (gaining agreement on business terms associated with any third-party suppliers)

4.   Marketing activities for a new product

    a.   Financial acumen (understanding business case financials)

    b.   Negotiation (identifying and resolving key issues between marketing and operations)

    c.   Communications (bridging discussions between operations and marketing)

Though four very different work experiences are listed above, the key skills utilized by George across these work experiences are similar. This situation is more often the rule than the exception since each individual tends to use the same existing skills repeatedly, relying on and honing a particular set of skills, often to the detriment of developing new skills.

George will take the output of this discussion and list all of his skills and their proficiency level using the same scale (1 to 10) as in Step 1. Here is George's list in order of proficiency:

George's Key Skill	Rating (1–10)
Negotiation	9
Communications (written and verbal)	8
Technical expertise	8
Financial acumen (knowledge of operational impacts on financials)	7
Prioritization	6
PM software proficiency	0

If you have worked with George for a while or have other insights into his key skills, you may need to discuss these ratings with him. The goal is to get an honest reflection of his skill set but you're only looking to be directionally correct. You don't want to spend hours determining if his financial acumen skills are a 6.2 or a 7.4.

Step 3: **Map** the two lists to determine an inventory of key skill gaps.

At this point, you have two lists; the list of skills and the associated proficiency level required to achieve job success and the list of skills and the associated proficiency level George possesses:

Key Skill	Rating (1–10)	
	Job Required	George
Communications (written and verbal)	10	8
Financial acumen (knowledge of operational impacts on financials)	8	7
PM software proficiency	7	0
Prioritization	7	6
Negotiation	7	9
Technical expertise	Not Required	8

By mapping these two lists, you can determine the skill proficiency gap (if any) between the skills required by the job and the skills possessed by George. You do this by subtracting the Job Required rating from the rating George gave himself for each skill. In the cases where George's skill rates less than the Job Required rating, you have a negative number that represents the size of the key skill gap. In cases where George's skill rates higher than the Job Required rating, you have a positive number that indicates you don't need to do any coaching in that area. In cases where George possesses a skill not needed for the job, he has an additional skill.

The output from mapping the two lists is as follows:

Job Required Key Skill	Proficiency Gap
PM software proficiency	-7
Communications (written and verbal)	-2
Financial acumen (knowledge of operational impacts on financials)	-1
Prioritization	-1
Negotiation	+2

Additional Key Skill	Proficiency Gap
Technical expertise	+8

In summary, George will need to work on four key skills in the following order:

Job Required Key Skill	Proficiency Gap
PM software proficiency	-7
Communications (written and verbal)	-2
Financial acumen (knowledge of operational impacts on financials)	-1
Prioritization	-1

George also possesses a negotiation skill level that exceeds the level the job requires and has a high level of technical expertise not required for success in the PM role. You must list and quantify all of the key skills an individual possesses, not just those required by the job. Three reasons exist for this approach:

1. You gain a complete picture of an individual's set of skills. You can leverage this knowledge to assist you in achieving your overall team goals. Simply put, George may be in the wrong job on your team. He may be a perfect fit for a technology job on your team that has nothing to do with project management but everything to do with negotiating complex technical contracts.

2. George may be able to consult with or coach another team member on a particular skill. In this example, George may be able to assist or coach a team member who is looking to improve their technical skills in the area where George has technical expertise.

3. If George is unable to achieve success in his current job, you can use the results of this mapping exercise to identify potential opportunities in other organizations where he can best use his skill set. In this case, you can share the mapping exercise with prospective organizations as a way to demonstrate you're

not looking to pass on a low-performing individual but, rather, you're looking for an opportunity to move a team member into a role in which he or she would be a better fit. This type of approach will benefit the company by having George maximize the use of his existing skills, and benefit you by helping build your reputation, as I explained in Chapter Two. Please note, that this approach only makes sense in cases where the individual merits this consideration due to their attitude and motivation.

At this point, we have completed the **Map** phase of MOST. You have determined and prioritized the key skills that George needs to improve to succeed in his PM role. You're ready to progress to the next phase of the coaching framework; **Order**, where we will determine the resources available to you to close these known key skill gaps.

Key takeaways

1. You must differentiate skill from _____.

2. _____ rate the proficiency of each required job skill.

3. The **Map** phase has three steps:

    a. Determine and list the _____ key skills and _____ proficiency level.

    b. Determine and list the _____ key skills and proficiency level.

    c. **Map** the two lists to determine an _____ of key skill gaps.

The answers are on page 134.

Chapter Five:

ORDER

Once you have a **Map** of the key skills that the individual needs to improve to succeed in their role, you need to determine the most effective resources available to you to close any identified gaps in those skills. This selection of resources is the second, or **Order,** phase of MOST™.

I use the term **Order** to imply a level of complexity beyond determining and obtaining the resource. Given the speed of business and the focus on cost and efficiency, you have to consider such factors as how much you spend for the resource, in what priority to use any resource, how much of any one resource you use and how you integrate different resources.

The **Order** phase is comprised of three specific steps used to determine and prioritize the resources that close key skill gaps.

Phase 2: **Order**

Order the resources that close key skill gaps.

Step 1: Create a list of all potential resources.
Step 2: Create a resource matrix for each skill gap.
Step 3: Prioritize the resources that best balance cost against impact.

To provide clarity, I will describe all three steps and illustrate these steps with an example at the end of the chapter.

Step 1: Create a list of all potential resources.

As you look to create a list of potential resources, you should note that a single resource may address multiple skill gaps, or you may need multiple resources to close a single skill gap. A sample of resources available to you includes, but is not limited to, the following:

1. Professional trainer
2. Job shadowing
3. Internal training programs
4. External training programs
5. Special assignments
6. Public speaking
7. Volunteer work
8. Reading

As you think through the resources at your disposal, I want to reiterate that the person you are coaching has to own the coaching plan. To that end, this individual needs to lead the efforts in thinking through prospective resources available to assist him or her in closing their key skill gap(s).

As the coach, you have the responsibility to provide a coaching framework and environment that provides the person you are coaching the opportunity to succeed. As part of that responsibility, you have to determine how motivated the individual is to succeed. If you are in a situation where the person you are coaching is not motivated, you still use the MOST framework to create a coaching plan, but you may have to take a more direct role in each phase of MOST, and you may have to limit the resources available to you in the coaching plan. For example, job shadowing, special assignments, volunteer work, training that requires an investment on the part of the company (such as formal coaching or training classes), and other skill development opportunities that require investment or unsupervised activities may be inappropriate for the individual who lacks motivation. A practical coach knows where to invest and where not to invest the company's resources.

Step 2: Create a resource matrix for each skill gap.

Once you have come up with a list of all of the available resources, you need to create a matrix to classify each resource based upon its relative cost (X-axis) and its relative impact (Y-axis) on closing the skill gap. You need to create a resource matrix for each skill gap. By doing so, you can focus on the best way to close each specific skill gap.

Before we create the matrices, we must remember we are always looking to be a practical coach. Being practical means we strive to understand all of the costs and impacts associated with using a resource, but we don't need to spend hours determining the exact costs and impacts. We need to understand relative cost and impact.

The output from each matrix will assist you with Step 3 when you look to understand the relative value that each resource brings to closing the collective skill gaps and the overall cost/impact of each resource. Once we understand relative value, we can factor in our cost limitations to finalize our decision on what resource(s) to employ.

In the following matrix (Figure 1), I classify each resource, based upon its relative cost (X-axis) and impact (Y-axis) on closing a defined skill gap.

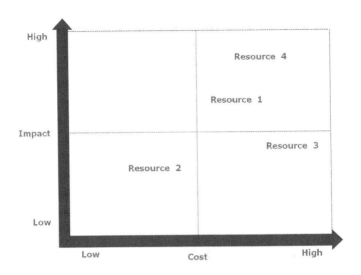

Figure 1: Example of a resource matrix to close a defined skill gap

The focus on creating this matrix is to illustrate that Resource 4 is more costly but has a greater impact on closing the defined skill gap that any of the other resources. To continue this example, Resource 2, while the least costly, also has the least impact on closing the defined skill gap.

Step 3: Prioritize the resources that best balance cost against impact.

In this step, you take the prioritized list of key skill gaps and the output from the resource matrices to determine which resources provide you the best collective cost/impact to close your skill gap(s).

Cost/impact balance is very important to the integrity of MOST. You want to select only those resources that have the greatest impact on the key skill gaps you need to close for the least cost. Least cost doesn't mean little or no cost. In some cases, the most expensive resource is essential, and though expensive, it may be the least costly as it is the only resource that impacts the skill gap you are trying to close.

Additionally, a resource that is relatively expensive but assists in closing all of the known skill gaps may provide more cost/impact than a single less expensive resource that closes only one skill gap. Lastly, you may find you do not have to utilize all or even most of the resources you listed in Step 1 if a single resource can meet all of your needs.

Now that we have a framework for the activities associated with the **Order** phase, I will work through an example using George in his PM role.

<u>George</u>
<u>PM Role</u>

<u>Phase 2: **Order**</u>

Step 1: Create a list of all potential resources.

Earlier in this chapter, we created a list of resources and we will assume they are available to assist George with closing his key skill gaps. These resources were the following:

1. Professional trainer
2. Job shadowing
3. Internal training programs
4. External training programs
5. Special assignments
6. Public speaking
7. Volunteer work
8. Reading

Let's examine each resource.

1.   Professional Trainer

The hiring of a professional trainer, someone additional to the organization who comes in and provides skills development training, can pay a number of dividends. You not only get someone with a singular focus and expertise in a particular area, but you may also arrange coaching sessions for multiple individuals who have the need to develop the same skill. A professional trainer should have a mix of real-world experience and training in the specific skills George needs to improve.

These types of formal training arrangements can be costly. Depending on the organization's size, you may be able to approach others outside your direct line of responsibility for funding or leverage programs run and paid for by the HR team within your organization.

If you can obtain the services of a professional trainer, you should brief the trainer on the MOST program as well as the **Map** work you have done so he or she can create or modify the training plan to meet the goals identified using the MOST framework.

2.   Job shadowing

There may be an opportunity for George to work directly with another employee on a deliverable, effectively shadowing that employee. When looking at these opportunities, four points need to be covered to ensure effective learning is accomplished:

a.   George should review the process documentation associated with the job. This is done for two reasons:
  i.   George needs to share with you how this assignment will provide exposure to the specific skill(s) he needs to improve and, thus, confirm this assignment fits his coaching plan.

ii. Few individuals know their job 100% or possess a skill at the 100% level. This means the person George is working with can't pass on 100% of the job knowledge or skill. By reviewing the process documentation before commencing the job shadowing, George can learn about the processes and skills associated with the job before seeing them in practice. In simple terms, watching a cook prepare a pie is one thing but reading about how to make a pie and then watching the cook prepare a pie creates a more tangible and complete learning experience.

b. If George is going to work with someone outside his organization, that person needs to know the purpose of George's assignment down to the level of agreeing on what activities George will perform, how his success is measured, and how feedback will be provided to you, the coach.

c. You will need to ensure the time allotted to George in his assignment is long enough for him to learn the needed skill(s) and practice them.

d.   You must ensure the other organization and individual benefit from working with George. You don't want to create a situation where the other organization and individual feel that working with George is a burden that could somehow jeopardize their success. One way to address this issue is to look for opportunities for sharing expertise. For example, George may need exposure to financial analysis methodologies, but as we know, he has excellent technical skills. You may be able to find an opportunity with someone who is willing to work with George on financial analysis methodologies in exchange for the opportunity to learn about a particular technical field. This type of arrangement benefits all parties.

In summary, if you want to maximize the benefits of job shadowing you need to invest sufficient time in the process. It is not simply a question of dumping someone into another organization for three hours a day over a two-week period. You and George have to identify appropriate opportunities and then ensure George and the individual in the receiving organization benefit from any job shadowing activities.

3.   Internal training programs

Many organizations have a list of their training programs that focus on skill development. If George wants to take a training program, he should list the specific skill(s) impacted by the program and reach an agreement with you on how the program will improve his overall performance and how that performance impact is measured. Otherwise, you can waste your budget on training programs that add little value once George puts the training handbook on the shelf and hangs his Certificate of Achievement in his workspace.

4.   External training programs

The selection of a training program offered by a third party needs to follow the same guidelines as the selection of an internal training program. In the case of these external training programs, it can be more difficult to ensure the content matches your specific needs and delivers the impact you expect. To that end, you should determine if your HR department has any experience with the program you are considering. If your HR department has no experience with the program or you don't have an HR department, ensure you research the program before sending anyone for training. Unlike most internal training programs, these programs are not free, so you need to ensure you don't waste time and money on a program that has little, if any, impact on the key skill gap.

5.   Special assignments

Special assignments are generally projects that fall outside of the individual's current area of responsibility. Aside from helping close a key skill gap, special assignments are often a reward and a challenge for high performing and high potential individuals as they provide exposure across the organization and thus increase potential for advancement. If you are looking to assign George a special assignment, you need to take into account three factors:

a.   The position the person holds
b.   The type of skill gap that needs to be closed
c.   The amount of exposure associated with the assignment

When selecting special assignments, you need to pay attention to the position the person holds. If George is a mid-level manager who has a number of people reporting to him, it may not encourage the appropriate response in George if he is given the special assignment of ordering paper products for the copier; even in the case where George needs to be build his logistical skills. As we discussed in Chapter Three, respect is one of the three guiding principles of MOST. To that end, ensure the special assignment does not put the individual in an embarrassing situation.

Special assignments must close a known skill gap. We know George possesses strong technical expertise, a skill unneeded in his PM role. To that end, putting George in charge of creating technical bulletins for another organization will not help close a known skill gap.

Lastly, certain special assignments can provide a significant amount of exposure for individuals as they work to close a skill gap. You want to avoid putting George in a situation where failure to close the key skill gap quickly enough could negatively impact the success of the high profile special assignment and damage George's career aspirations.

6.   Public Speaking

I have worked with many individuals who have excellent ideas but cannot present them effectively to an audience, whether it is two people across the conference table or a room full of customers at a convention. In my experience, the person who cannot put across an excellent idea often lacks basic communication skills related to understanding his or her audience and its incentives. The key to an effective presentation is to ask two questions: "Who is my audience?" and "What do I want to tell them?" An effective presentation flows from answering these two questions. Public speaking provides the opportunity to practice these skills, usually in non-threatening forums. Although George has solid communications skills, he may still benefit from joining a club that teaches and encourages these communications skills.

7.   Volunteer work

Volunteer work can provide a relatively stress-free way for George to work on a skill set, but it is not something you as a coach can easily monitor or measure. Most volunteer work takes place outside of normal working hours, and linking improved job performance back to the volunteer effort can be difficult. If you and George agree to use volunteer work as one of your skill improvement activities, you need to take special care to determine and agree on how to measure the impact of this volunteer work on George's performance.

8.   Reading

Reading a book, periodical, or reference material is another way for George to access the information needed to close a skill gap. As with the training programs mentioned earlier, the key to using reading as a resource is to understand how you apply the information to the job and how you measure the impact. It's a good idea to have George write and present a book report giving an overview of the book's content, key insights, and ways to apply those insights to the job.

Step 2: Create a resource matrix for each skill gap.

Now that we have reviewed the list of resources available to assist George in closing his skill gaps, we will create a matrix to classify each resource based upon its relative cost (X-axis) and impact (Y-axis) on closing the skill gap.

The output from each matrix will assist you with Step 3 when you look to understand the relative value that each resource brings to closing the collective skill gaps and the overall cost/impact of each resource. Once we understand relative value, we can factor in our cost limitations to finalize our decision on what resource(s) to employ.

As you may recall from page 33, George needs to focus on closing the following key skill gaps:

Job Required Key Skill	Proficiency Gap
PM software proficiency	-7
Communications	-2
Financial acumen	-1
Prioritization	-1

We will create a resource matrix for each of these skill gaps.

PM software proficiency

In the following matrix (Figure 2), I classify each resource based upon its relative cost (X-axis) and impact (Y-axis) on closing the PM software proficiency skill gap.

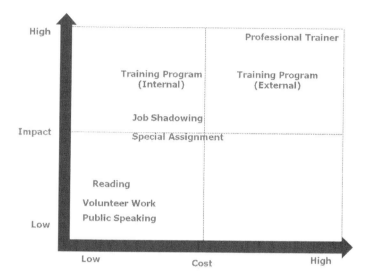

Figure 2: Resource matrix for PM software proficiency

The focus on creating this matrix is to build appropriate rigor into learning and leveraging the use of PM software.

It's fair to assume that the services of a professional trainer dedicated to one-on-one training provides the most impact but is more expensive than any other resource.

As I discussed earlier in the chapter, the internal training programs should be easier to review to ensure they meet your needs. These internal courses can be much less expensive than training programs available in the open market (external) and can be as effective.

Job shadowing can benefit George at a reasonable cost to the business with a special assignment judged a credible option.

When it comes to reading, this is a low-cost option but can be less effective than the previously discussed options.

Though public speaking and volunteer work cost you little or nothing, it does not seem obvious that either of these options provide an opportunity for George to close his PM software proficiency skill gap.

At this point, we have completed a matrix for the PM software proficiency skill gap and looking at the matrix through a cost/impact lens, it illustrates that an internal training program and a job shadowing opportunity provide the best options to close the PM software proficiency skill gap.

Communications

In the following matrix (Figure 3), I classify each resource based upon its relative cost (X-axis) and impact (Y-axis) on closing the communications skill gap.

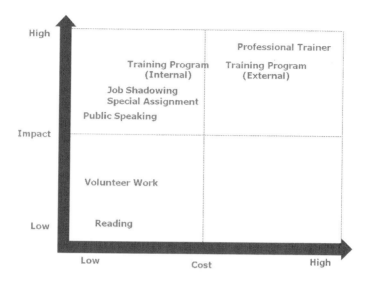

Figure 3: Resource matrix for communications

The focus on creating this matrix is to ensure George has the opportunity to interact with other project managers and, by doing so, gain the feedback and experience necessary to improve his communications skills.

A professional trainer and training programs can have more impact than other resources but are more costly and thus less cost effective.

Job shadowing, a special assignment, or public speaking provides George the opportunity to close this skill gap in a cost effective manner.

Though volunteer work provides George the opportunity to interact with others, it is hard to determine the quality of those interactions and their impact on closing this skill gap.

When it comes to reading, this is a low-cost option but its impact on closing the communications skill gap is considered minimal.

At this point, we have completed a matrix for the communications skill gap, and looking at the matrix through a cost/impact lens, it illustrates that job shadowing and a special assignment provide the best options to close the communications skill gap.

Financial acumen

In the following matrix (Figure 4), I classify each resource based upon its relative cost (X-axis) and impact (Y-axis) on closing the financial acumen skill gap.

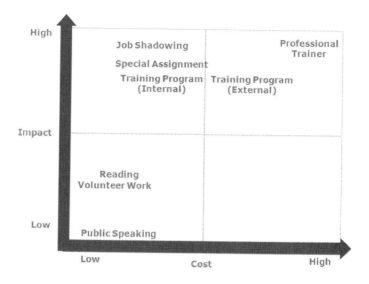

Figure 4: Resource matrix for financial acumen

The focus on creating this matrix is to ensure that George has the opportunity to work on forecasts, projections and financial calculations to improve his financial acumen skills.

As discussed with PM software skills, a professional trainer dedicated to one-on-one training is the most effective option to close this skill gap but also the most costly. Training programs are effective with the internal training program deemed the less expensive option.

Job shadowing and a special assignment provide the opportunities to develop financial acumen skills under the tutelage of fellow professionals.

Depending on the material selected, reading may provide some impact for little relative cost.

Volunteer work may provide the opportunity to learn financial acumen skills but ensuring George is learning the correct methods and procedures may be difficult.

Public speaking has no impact on this skill gap.

At this point, we have completed a matrix for the financial acumen skill gap and looking at the matrix through a cost/impact lens, it illustrates that job shadowing and a special assignment provide the best options to close the financial acumen skill gap.

Prioritization

In the following matrix (Figure 5), I classify each resource based upon its relative cost (X-axis) and impact (Y-axis) on closing the prioritization skill gap.

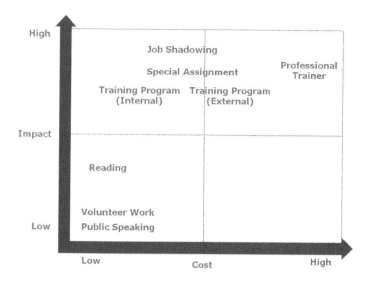

Figure 5: Resource matrix for prioritization

The focus on creating this matrix is to ensure that George has the opportunity to interact with other project managers and by doing so, gain the feedback and experience necessary to improve his ability to prioritize activities and decisions.

Job shadowing and a special assignment provide the most cost effective options for George to work on his prioritization skills.

A professional trainer will have an impact on this skill gap but he or she may not know how activities and decisions are prioritized in the organization and is more expensive than other options.

Internal and external training programs can be less effective than other options because they may not focus on the specific business issues of importance to George, and in most cases, external training programs are more costly than other options.

Depending on the material selected, reading may provide some impact for little cost.

Volunteer work and public speaking provide little, if any, measureable impact on closing this skill gap.

At this point, we have completed a matrix for the prioritization skill gap and looking at the matrix through a cost/impact lens, it illustrates that job shadowing and a special assignment provide the best cost/impact options to close the prioritization skill gap.

Step 3: Prioritize the resources that best balance cost against impact.

In this step, you take the prioritized list of key skill gaps and the output from the resource matrices to determine which resources provide you the best collective cost/impact to close your skill gaps.

As mentioned earlier, cost/impact balance is very important to the integrity of MOST. You want to select only those resources that have the greatest impact on the key skill gaps that George needs to close for the least cost. Least cost doesn't mean little or no cost. In some cases, the most expensive resource is essential and, though expensive, it may still be the least costly as it is the only resource that impacts the skill gap you want to close.

Additionally, an expensive resource that assists in closing all of the known skill gaps may provide more cost/impact than a single cheaper resource that closes only one skill gap. Lastly, you may find that you do not have to utilize all or even most of the resources that you came up with in Step 1 if a single resource can meet all of your needs.

We can now examine the skill gaps we need to close and the collective results from the resource matrices:

Job Required Key Skill	Proficiency Gap	Resource Matrix Results
PM software proficiency	-7	Internal training program and job shadowing
Communications	-2	Job shadowing and special assignment
Financial acumen	-1	Job shadowing and special assignment
Prioritization	-1	Job shadowing and special assignment

In summary, when we take into account that the PM software proficiency skill gap is the most important skill gap to close and that job shadowing impacts all four key skill gaps, the practical decision is to focus George's coaching plan in two areas:

1. An internal training course that focuses on PM software proficiency skills
2. A job shadow opportunity

Given our decision above, the final use of resources will be as follows:

Job Required Key Skill	Proficiency Gap	Resource Matrix Results
PM software proficiency	-7	Internal training program and job shadowing
Communications	-2	Job shadowing
Financial acumen	-1	Job shadowing
Prioritization	-1	Job shadowing

I want to address two questions. The first question is why don't we focus our coaching plan on three items and include the special assignment? After all, the special assignment has impact across three of the four key skills. The answer is that we are being practical. As I state throughout the book, you are looking to balance cost and impact and cost includes time and effort. With an internal training program and job shadowing, you have two resources that address all of the skill gaps with a focus on the most important skill gap, PM software proficiency. These resources dovetail nicely together since you can start the job shadowing right after you complete the training course. Setting up a special assignment would take additional time, effort and resources, and it doesn't address the most important skill gap. In the end, the practical decision is to focus on only two resources.

The second question is do we have to use four separate job shadow resources to address the four key skill gaps? The answer is no for the same reason as above: We are being practical. Keeping George busy in four separate job shadow activities is as impractical as managing four separate job shadow relationships. In this case, you will look for a PM who has excellent skills using the selected PM software as well as appropriate skills in the areas of communication, financial acumen, and prioritization. Though it may be impossible to find a PM who is a match with all of these skills, you should prioritize your selection of a PM in order of their proficiency with the selected PM software, and then their skills in the area of communications, financial acumen, and prioritization.

At this point, we have completed the **Order** phase of MOST. You have determined the most effective resources available to you to close the defined skill gaps. You're ready to progress to the next phase of the MOST coaching framework: **Structure**. In that phase, we will integrate all of the information we have collected into a structured coaching plan.

Key takeaways

1. _____ is a key theme in the **Order** phase of MOST.
2. You need to be able to _____ the impact of any resource that you employ.
3. Least cost doesn't mean _____ cost.

The answers are on page 135.

Chapter Six:

STRUCTURE

You have created a **Map** of the key skill gaps you need to close and an **Order** for the resources you are going to use to close those skill gaps. The third phase in the MOST™ framework is to **Structure** a coaching plan.

As with all phases of MOST, we want to be efficient with time and money. In the **Structure** phase of MOST, efficiency means focusing on the activity we are going to perform, the tangible output expected from that activity, and the measureable impact on key metrics. I use the term bridge or bridging to illustrate the linked relationship between activity, output, and impact.

In the **Structure** phase of MOST, the key guiding principle is: Set goals. Settings goals can be a very difficult task. You must be able to balance the needs of the business with the setting of goals that are achievable. Depending on the rationale behind the coaching plan, the individual may be dealing with some feelings of insecurity and setting goals that are seen as unachievable will make it very difficult to keep the individual motivated. To that end, you need to have open communications regarding the selection and alignment of activities, outputs, and impacts.

The **Structure** phase of MOST involves three specific steps to create a coaching plan.

Phase 3: **Structure**

> **Structure** a coaching plan.
>
> Step 1: Create a list of activities associated with each resource.
> Step 2: List the expected outputs from performing any activity.
> Step 3: Determine the impact on the key business metric.

To provide clarity, I will describe all three steps and illustrate all three steps with an example at the end of the chapter.

> Step 1: Create a list of activities associated with each resource.

Once we have selected a set of resources in the **Order** phase of MOST, we need to understand the discrete activities associated with using each resource. No set ratio exists between the resource and the number of discrete activities associated with using that resource. For example, if you are going to read a book, you may have only two discrete activities: selecting and reading the book. You want to focus on the key activities associated with employing a resource and to list as few or as many as appropriate.

> Step 2: List the expected outputs from performing any activity.

Activities bridge to outputs. As in Step 1, no set ratio exists between activities and outputs. A single activity can have a single output or multiple outputs. To continue our example, there are two activities associated with reading a book and there may be two outputs: writing a book report and making a presentation on how to apply the lessons learned from the book.

> Step 3: Determine the impact on the key business metric.

You must agree on how the outputs associated with each activity impact the key metrics. This can be a difficult process particularly in cases where multiple activities generate multiple outputs that all impact the same key metric. Knowing the exact impact of each individual activity on each key metric may be impossible to calculate. However, as I stated at the start of this book, I am looking to provide a common-sense approach to the coaching process, a process that involves a series of interactions and a balance between cost and impact. You need to use this common-sense approach and not complex mathematical models to determine impacts on key metrics.

Now that we have a framework for the activities associated with the **Structure** phase, I will work through an example using George in his PM role.

<u>George</u>
<u>PM Role</u>

Phase 3: **Structure**

As you may recall from the **Map** and **Order** phases, we learned about George and his skill gaps and the resources available to close those skill gaps. We determined we were going to structure George's coaching plan on two resources: an internal training program and job shadowing.

Job Required Key Skill	Proficiency Gap	Resource Matrix Results
PM software proficiency	-7	Internal training program and job shadowing
Communications	-2	Job shadowing
Financial acumen	-1	Job shadowing
Prioritization	-1	Job shadowing

Internal training program

Job Required Key Skill	Proficiency Gap	Resource Matrix Results
PM software proficiency	-7	Internal training program

Step 1: Create a list of activities associated with each resource.

1.   Complete an entry-level course on the required software package

Step 2: List the expected outputs from performing any activity.

1.   Certified completion of the course
2.   Bi-weekly project status report using the software package including details on budget, resource management, project management targets, and key milestones

Step 3: Determine the impact on the key business metric.

1.   On time: Projects complete within 2% of target completion date
2.   On budget: Projects complete within 5% of budget

As stated earlier in the chapter, determining the exact impact of any activity on a key metric can be difficult. However, you can determine a reasonable expectation for improvement based upon business objectives. In this case, George and his coach have agreed that completing projects within 2% of the target completion date and 5% of the budget are achievable goals.

Job shadowing

Job Required Key Skill	Proficiency Gap	Resource Matrix Results
PM software proficiency	-7	Job shadowing
Communications	-2	Job shadowing
Financial acumen	-1	Job shadowing
Prioritization	-1	Job shadowing

Step 1: Create a list of activities associated with each resource.

1. Selection and introduction of PM for job shadowing

The selection and introduction of the PM will occur after George completes the PM software proficiency course. Job shadowing will last a period of six months during which time George will spend one half-day every two weeks with the selected PM.

As I stated at the end of the previous chapter, keeping George busy in four separate job shadow activities is as impractical as managing four separate job shadow relationships. In this case, you will look for a PM who has excellent skills using the selected PM software as well as appropriate skills in the areas of communication, financial acumen, and prioritization. Though it may be impossible to find a PM who is a match with all of these skills, you should prioritize your selection of a PM in order of their proficiency with the selected PM software, and then their skills in the area of communications, financial acumen, and prioritization.

Step 2: List the expected outputs from performing any activity.

1. Start and finish dates for job shadowing activities
2. One-page report on lessons learned the day after each job shadow session with focus on how to incorporate the lessons learned into his PM reports
3. George will lead bi-weekly project calls across key stakeholder organizations and solicit active participation and feedback from represented organizations driving to a consensus on key financial decisions, priorities, deliverables, and timelines

4.   Provide bi-weekly detailed meeting minutes and tracking of outstanding action items
5.   The manager who is being shadowed must provide monthly feedback on George using a simple checklist that covers such topics as ability to listen, willingness to participate, and work output

Step 3: Determine the impact on the key business metric.

1.   On time: Projects complete within 2% of target completion date
2.   On budget: Projects complete within 5% of budget
3.   Client satisfaction survey scores on George increase 10%

George and his coach have earlier agreed that completing projects within 2% of the target completion date and 5% of the budget reflect the impact of taking an internal training course. Job shadowing complements the internal training course and impacts the same key metrics. Given the complementary nature of these two resources, we will consider the impact on the key metrics is a collective 2% on the target completion date and 5% on the budget. Job shadowing will provide George the opportunity to work on his communication, financial acumen, and prioritization skills, and these efforts are expected to improve his client satisfaction scores by 10%.

In summary, the impact of applying these two resources to close George's skill gaps are that projects will be completed within 2% of the target completion date and 5% of the target budget, with a 10% improvement in his client satisfaction scores.

At this point, we have completed the **Structure** phase of MOST. You have created a list of activities to be performed, the tangible output expected from each activity, and the measureable impact on key metrics. You're now ready to progress to the final phase of the MOST coaching framework; **Track**. In that phase, we will create a tracking template to ensure the success of the structured coaching plan.

Key takeaways

1. _____: Is the key guiding principle of the **Structure** phase of MOST.
2. You need to bridge _____ to _____ and _____ to _____.
3. You use a _____ approach to determine the impact on key metrics.

The answers are on page 135.

Chapter Seven:

TRACK

This phase of MOST™, **Track**, coalesces all of the effort you've put into the earlier phases of the framework (**Map**, **Order**, and **Structure**) to generate a tracking template. The tracking template ensures you stay focused on achieving outputs and the associated impacts on the key metrics.

The **Track** phase of MOST is comprised of three specific steps that lead to the creation of a tracking template.

Phase 4: **Track**

Track the results.

Step 1: Consolidate the outputs and impacts from the **Structure** phase.

Step 2: Assign start and end dates to each output and impact.

Step 3: Create a tracking template.

To provide clarity, I will describe all three steps and illustrate all three steps with an example at the end of the chapter.

> Step 1: Consolidate the outputs and impacts from the **Structure** phase.

The collective outputs and impacts from Steps 2 and 3 of the **Structure** phase of MOST are the milestones you will need to track. As you list the outputs and impacts, you may find you have multiple iterations of the same output or impact. This can happen if more than one resource addresses a single skill gap. If this occurs, you can eliminate duplicate items when you create a consolidated list of outputs and impacts.

> Step 2: Assign start and end dates to each output and impact.

As you look to assign start and end dates to each output and impact, you will need to consider six factors:

1. Ensure that you prioritize the completion of outputs by importance.
2. As you assign start and end dates, allow for sufficient time for the individual to practice and improve his or her skill(s). Few people

can take instruction and maximize that instruction's value with little or no practice.

3. Are any of your outputs dependent upon other outputs? If so, you need to account for this dependency when you assign your start and end dates.

4. Constraints may exist on the ability to practice certain skills. You may operate in a business environment where you perform certain activities only at specific times of the year. You will need to incorporate the timing of these business cycles into your start and end dates.

5. What is the impact of the coaching plan on overall workload? Even though discrete activities may last only a few days or weeks, a complete coaching plan may last for months. Make sure your timelines incorporate the individuals need to perform their core work duties along with the activities associated with the coaching plan.

6. Some outputs may have a start date with a recurring end date that remains unspecified. For example, you may require a report at the end of each project, but you don't know when each project will end. In these cases, you need to note that the report is due at some specific interval such as the end of each project.

Step 3: Create a tracking template.

The coaching associated with MOST is a process, not a one-time event, so a tracking template ensures focus on the outputs and impacts on key metrics. The tracking template can be as simple or as complicated as you need. You can write the dates on a calendar, make a checklist on a notepad or create a project plan using a project management software package. The template format is unimportant, what is important is that you have a way to ensure outputs occur when required and metrics are meeting goals.

Now that we have a framework for the activities associated with the **Track** phase, I will work through an example using George in his PM role.

<u>George</u>
<u>PM Role</u>

<u>Phase 4: **Track**</u>

Step 1: Consolidate the outputs and impacts from the **Structure** phase.

We know from the **Structure** phase that we are going to utilize two resources in George's coaching plan: an internal training program and job shadowing.

Internal training program

Job Required Key Skill	Proficiency Gap	Resource Matrix Results
PM software proficiency	-7	Internal training program

Outputs

1. Certified completion of the course
2. Bi-weekly project status report using the software package including details on budget, resource management, project management targets, and key milestones

Impacts

1. On time: Projects complete within 2% of target completion date
2. On budget: Projects complete within 5% of budget

Job shadowing

Job Required Key Skill	Proficiency Gap	Resource Matrix Results
PM software proficiency	-7	Job shadowing
Communications	-2	Job shadowing
Financial acumen	-1	Job shadowing
Prioritization	-1	Job shadowing

Outputs

1. Start and finish dates for job shadowing activities
2. One-page report on lessons learned the day after each job shadow session with focus on how to incorporate the lessons learned into his PM reports
3. George will lead bi-weekly project calls across key stakeholder organizations and solicit active participation and feedback from represented organizations driving to a consensus on key financial decisions, priorities, deliverables, and timelines
4. Provide bi-weekly detailed meeting minutes and tracking of outstanding action items
5. The manager who is being shadowed must provide monthly feedback on George using a simple checklist that covers such topics as ability to listen, willingness to participate, and work output

Impacts

1. On time: Projects complete within 2% of tar-
    get completion date
2. On budget: Projects complete within 5% of budget
3. Client satisfaction survey scores on George
    increase 10%

As we consolidate all the outputs and impacts and
eliminate duplicated items, we have a finalized list of
what we need to track:

Consolidated Outputs

1. Certified completion of the course
2. Start and finish dates for job shadowing ac-
    tivities
3. One-page report on lessons learned the day
    after each job shadow session with focus on
    how to incorporate the lessons learned into his
    PM reports
4. Bi-weekly project status report using the soft-
    ware package including details on budget,
    resource management, project management
    targets, and key milestones
5. George will lead bi-weekly project calls
    across key stakeholder organizations and so-
    licit active participation and feedback from

represented organizations driving to a consensus on key financial decisions, priorities, deliverables, and timelines

6. Provide bi-weekly detailed meeting minutes and tracking of outstanding action items

7. The manager who is being shadowed must provide monthly feedback on George using a simple checklist that covers such topics as ability to listen, willingness to participate, and work output

Consolidated Impacts

1. On time: Projects complete within 2% of target completion date

2. On budget: Projects complete within 5% of budget

3. Client satisfaction survey scores on George increase 10%

Step 2: Assign start and end dates to each output and impact.

As we look to assign start and end dates, we know the training program is the highest priority item, and all other outputs are subordinate to it. To that end, the start date of the training course becomes Day 1 (regardless of the calendar date) for your tracking template, and all other outputs are subordinate to that date. For this example, I have made four assumptions:

1. The PM course is four weeks in length, or 20 business days, and starts on a Monday
2. The first report using the software occurs five business days after completion of the course
3. The first bi-weekly project call starts 10 business days after completing the course
4. Job shadowing starts on a Monday, 15 business days after the completion of the course

Using the above assumptions, we get the following dates for George's coaching plan:

1. Start and end date of PM software course: Day 1 to Day 26
2. Start date of bi-weekly project status reports: Day 33; recurring every 10 business days
3. Start date of bi-weekly project calls: Day 40; recurring every 10 business days
4. Start date of bi-weekly meeting minutes: Day 40; recurring every 10 business days
5. Start and end date of job shadowing sessions: Day 50 to Day 201

6.   Start and end date of job shadow lessons learned: Day 51; recurring every 10 business days

7.   Start and end date of job shadow feedback report: Day 82; recurring every month

8.   At completion of project:

    a.   Confirm project completion within 2% of target completion date

    b.   Confirm project completion within 5% of budget

    c.   Confirm client satisfaction survey score improvement of 10%

Step 3: Create a tracking template.

As George is working to improve his PM skills, we will use a PM software program as our tracking template. We will enter all start and end dates into our tracking template. A number of outputs occur many times over the six-month period associated with job shadowing and George needs to enter all of the outputs and impacts into the PM software program. However, for brevity, I will only illustrate entries for outputs and impacts that occur within the first 100 days:

Day	Entry
1	Start of PM course
26	End of PM course
33	Start of bi-weekly project status report
40	Start of bi-weekly project calls and meeting minutes
47	Bi-weekly status report
50	Start of job shadowing sessions
51	Job shadowing lessons learned
54	Bi-weekly project calls and meeting minutes
61	Bi-weekly status report
64	Job shadowing session
65	Job shadowing lessons learned
68	Bi-weekly project calls and meeting minutes
75	Bi-weekly status report
78	Job shadowing session
79	Job shadowing lessons learned
82	Bi-weekly project calls, meeting minutes and first report from job shadowing manager
89	Bi-weekly status report
92	Job shadowing session
93	Job shadowing lessons learned
96	Bi-weekly project calls and meeting minutes

If any project completes during this first 100-day period, you will need to note the following:

1. Confirm project completion within 2% of target completion date
2. Confirm project completion within 5% of budget
3. Confirm client satisfaction survey score improvement of 10%

Congratulations. You and George have completed all four phases of MOST. You now have a practical and structured coaching plan focused on the improvement of the key skills that impact results, and you have a tracking template to ensure you stay focused on your plan.

Key takeaways

1. Eliminate _____ items when you consolidate outputs and impacts.
2. Coaching is not a _____event.
3. Tracking templates don't need to be _____.

The answers are on page 135.

Chapter Eight:
IMPLEMENTING MOST™

As you look to implement MOST™ within your organization, you will need to educate, build consensus, and overcome any objections with key stakeholders. With MOST, the key stakeholders are your leadership team, the first team member with whom you plan to implement MOST and the remaining members of your team.

Leadership team

We all know that change, any change, can be difficult. We also know that the larger the organization, the more difficult it can be to implement change, no matter how small. For this reason, when you talk with your leadership team about implementing MOST, you must stress the flexibility of the MOST framework, specifically as it relates to the existing performance evaluation process.

Implementing MOST does not mean you are discarding or working around your existing employee performance evaluation processes. MOST is not an evaluation process but a framework used to identify and close skill gaps impeding the achievement of current performance goals. As such, MOST supports any evaluation process.

This plug-in nature of MOST means that even in organizations with heavily regulated evaluation processes, such as unionized environments, negotiating changes to any evaluation process or objective is unnecessary. For example, strict rules may exist concerning the selection and measurement of performance metrics such as Revenue per Call or Units Sold per Quarter. Implementing MOST does not require you to change these performance metrics or the way you measure these performance metrics. MOST does provide the framework to determine and improve the skills that impact your Revenue per Call or Units Sold per Quarter.

When you emphasize that you're not looking to change any existing evaluation process but want to employ a coaching framework focused on using skill development to drive performance improvement, most leadership teams will support your approach.

That said, even implementing a change of this type raises comments and questions. The three most often raised comments or questions are as follows:

1. Use the existing coaching process.
2. We don't have any additional money for a new coaching framework.
3. How long will the MOST coaching framework take to get results?

If you're given the opportunity to respond to these kind of comments and questions, I would respond as follows:

1. Use the existing coaching process.

The existing coaching process is not working as well as you'd like for certain individuals on your team. Therefore, you want to use MOST to determine key skill gaps and create an action plan more tailored to individuals and their specific needs. You see MOST as an opportunity to augment the tools available to you to drive performance improvement.

2. We don't have any additional money for a new coaching framework.

You need no additional funding. The resources currently available to the organization related to performance management are sufficient; they will simply be allocated using the MOST framework.

3.   How long will the MOST coaching framework take to get results?

This is the most difficult question to answer since you don't yet know. What you do know is the current coaching process is not providing you the results you want or need. Even though you will be unable to provide an exact timeline as you haven't yet implemented MOST, you can let your leadership team know that by implementing MOST, you will be able to provide a comprehensive timeline on the actions you take and the results you generate using a tracking template.

The leadership teams I have been involved with have all had the same approach to addressing issues of performance: They want to see an action plan and they want to see results. If you propose an approach to coaching that focuses on driving results, you will rarely be told you cannot do it, especially if you emphasize you are not asking them to change any official evaluation process and you are not asking for any additional funding.

Individual team member

You should review the performance of each member of your team and select an individual who will most benefit from the implementation of MOST.

Do you select an individual who is a top performer who needs to grow a certain skill to be ready for promotion?

Do you work with a new employee who may be highly motivated but who isn't learning the details of the job quickly enough?

Do you work with an individual who has been in the job for some time but whose performance isn't up to the standard?

While you will be using the same MOST framework for each individual, as I discussed in Chapter Six (**Structure**), the coaching plan associated with each of these individuals will be unique.

Selecting the top performer who needs to grow a certain skill to be ready for promotion is not always the clear or easy choice for the initial rollout of MOST. In my experience, coaching highly motivated, goal-oriented individuals provides its own unique challenges. These individuals generally have strong opinions, are willing to challenge the status quo and new ideas, and want to influence decisions and outcomes as much as possible. Simply put, there is no more or less work associated with coaching a top performer than coaching a low performer.

Once you have selected a team member to work with, you need to sit down with him or her and talk through the MOST framework and approach. You should cover three key points in your initial discussion:

1. The performance evaluation process remains the same

No matter whom you work with, the first point you must make is that the performance evaluation process remains the same. No one wants to be the guinea pig for a new performance evaluation process you thought up no matter how much he or she may respect or like you. Each individual must know that MOST is not a new evaluation process but a framework used to identify and close skill gaps and improve performance and results.

2. Discuss their definition of success

Whenever I enter into a coaching relationship, the first question I ask the individual I am coaching is to define success for their career, not the current job or the specific coaching relationship.

Does this sound simplistic? The first time you talk with someone about implementing a coaching relationship, you're supposed to ask them to define success for their entire career. What if they don't know? What if they tell you that they hate their job and want to move to Iceland and study volcanoes? What if they don't tell you the truth but tell you what they think you want to hear? The most important part of this interaction is that you ask the question and listen to the answer. In all cases, the goal is to begin a dialogue about their definition of success.

If they have no answer, you can begin a dialogue by talking about what they think defines success in their current role.

For the person who wants to move to Iceland, you can discuss how their current job is helping them achieve their goal.

For the individual who tells you what they think you want to hear, the process can be more complicated. A relationship that begins with someone telling you what they think you want to hear isn't going to get any better until an element of trust can be established. That trust begins with the individual understanding that you're asking the question because you are interested in them as a person, not a resource.

The ensuing dialogue around this question helps you understand the individual's perception of their performance and career aspirations. For example, an individual with a history of poor performance, who tells you they want to be a division president in two years, represents a different set of coaching issues than the top performer who may not have thought about career advancement or professional development opportunities in other organizations.

One caveat about asking this question: Give people as much time as possible to think about their answer. Let people know this is a fundamental question about their performance, their goals and their career aspirations.

Am I saying you need to ask the individual you are coaching this one question and all of a sudden, any issues you have with their performance or motivation will simply vanish? No. What I am saying is that individuals are more engaged in any coaching plan when they feel they are working on something that helps them achieve their goals and not just something they need to do to help the organization or to keep their job. Asking this question is the best way I have found to lay the foundation for building respect in a relationship and aligning individual and organizational goals.

3.   MOST is a collaborative process.

The individual you're coaching needs to understand and appreciate that you're looking to develop and grow his or her skill set, and you will use a process called MOST to accomplish that task. At this point, you can provide a quick overview of the four MOST components; **Map**, **Order**, **Structure**, and **Track**.

As part of this discussion, you must communicate the underlying principles of MOST (Be respectful, Set goals, and Take ownership). You need to be clear that MOST is not about you the coach, doing all of the work. It is about the two of you working together with the individual taking ownership of the deliverables associated with each phase of MOST.

In my experience, when you provide an individual the opportunity for coaching and development tailored to their specific needs, and present the opportunity as described above, they embrace it. If, after these discussions the individual does not wish to make a commitment to the MOST coaching framework, you should ask specific questions about their objections.

The first question is to ask the individual to list all of his or her reasons why they don't want to try MOST. What you want to do is get this list on paper, make it tangible, and evaluate and address each issue. You want to avoid the continuous drip, drip, drip of reasons why the individual doesn't want to or can't engage. I have found that objections to MOST, or any coaching program, usually fall into one of two broad categories: I don't need to change or I don't have the time.

I would argue these objections are different words for the same thing - concern about change. People dislike change. They resist change and will often fight against it even when it benefits them. So, don't be discouraged. Concern about change is something you need to recognize and work toward eliminating. This takes us back again to the first principle of MOST: Be respectful. Let's discuss how to address this concern using two cases; the low performer needing to meet the job standard and the top performer needing to grow new skills to get to the next level.

In the case of the low performer, you'll want to focus the discussion on current results. Since the performance standard is set and the low performer isn't meeting the standard, a tangible need exists for the individual to change. Without change, performance will continue to fall short of the standard and not meeting the standard has consequences. This last comment is not a threat, but it does emphasize that the individual needs to change, and MOST can help bring about that change. The discussion should flow into how much time they are spending on activities to improve performance. If this individual (unbeknownst to you) is working on activities to improve performance, ask for the list of the activities he or she is undertaking and the time needed for those activities. You can determine how many, if any, of these activities fit into the MOST framework to help build the needed skill(s). The goal is to reach the point where you can illustrate the activities are or are not driving improvement in the appropriate skill and impacting results.

If the activities are helpful, look to incorporate them into the MOST framework.

If, after all of the discussions, they do not wish to utilize the MOST coaching framework, then the issue is not MOST, you have a motivation issue. As stated above, MOST is a collaborative process and given the time and effort that the individual will need to put into MOST, demanding that this individual engage in a coaching relationship using MOST is not the preferred way to gain their active participation. However, when you have an individual who is not meeting the performance goals for the organization, you need to do something.

You can terminate the individual's employment. Though this sounds easy, terminating an individual's employment is generally a long and complicated process in all but a handful of cases. Ironically, the termination process in most organizations often includes the requirement that you, as the supervisor, demonstrate that you have attempted some type of performance improvement coaching.

You can move the individual into a position within your organization where their lack of skill and motivation will have a reduced impact on results. The issue here is that it quickly becomes apparent to everyone in the organization that you moved this individual into a role where he or she is being rewarded with less work for performing at an unacceptable level. This approach will have long-term negative consequences on organizational morale and performance.

You can look to move this individual to another organization. I want to take this opportunity to clarify one of the benefits of MOST that I discussed on pages 34 and 35. Moving a motivated individual to another organization who has the key skills needed to succeed in that organization creates organizational efficiency. This move is good for the individual, good for your organization, and good for the other organization. Moving people across organizations who are not meeting organization goals and worse, are unmotivated to improve their skills, is "passing the bad penny". "Passing the bad penny" will tarnish your reputation. After all, you've either allowed someone to leave your organization or sold someone on taking an individual from your organization, whom you know is not meeting the standard and who is unmotivated to improve. Word will quickly filter out that you cannot be trusted when it becomes apparent that this individual is not only a poor performer but also someone who is not motivated to improve.

You can do nothing but hope this individual gets better. This is the worst option. The individual isn't performing at the required level and continues to negatively affect the team's results. Everyone on the team knows this individual is not performing at an acceptable level and observes you are not addressing the issue. As with the other approaches that don't involve taking a proactive stand on the issue of non-performance, this approach will have long-term negative consequences on organizational morale and performance.

If you are not going to terminate the employment of this individual, move them to a new role on your team, "pass the bad penny", or have them sit in a cubicle while you hope they miraculously improve, then you will need to coach them. If you are going to coach them, then the best way to determine how to drive their needed skill improvement is to use the MOST process. Though it's unfortunate this individual does not initially embrace MOST, you can start the process and look to build the coaching relationship as you work through MOST.

In the case of the top performer, you have the same two objections: I don't need to change or I don't have the time. I'll start with the discussion of time. The top performer may be overloaded with additional work requests from others in the organization because everyone knows this individual gets things done. The top performer may not have the time to engage in additional activities even if these activities focus on building a needed skill. If this is the case, the discussion takes the same form as that with the low performer. Ask the top performer to provide you a list of the additional activities he or she is undertaking and the time needed for those activities. You can determine how many, if any, of these additional activities fit into the MOST framework to help build the needed skill(s).

As for the second objection, if this individual doesn't want to grow his or her skill set and is, by definition, doing the job at a high level, you don't need them to embrace a coaching relationship using MOST. Having a top performer on your team who only wants to keep performing the same job at a high level is fine. Remember, one of the benefits of using the **Map** phase of MOST is you become more efficient with your coaching time. Using MOST to identify team members you don't have to formally coach is an appropriate use of the process.

Team members

Now that you have organizational and individual alignment to begin using MOST, you need to brief your entire team. This takes us back to the first principle of MOST: Be respectful. Your team members know who is and who is not meeting or exceeding their performance goals. They will be talking about what you, the leader, are or are not doing about individual performance, accountability and overall team performance.

By briefing all of your team members on MOST, you make them aware of the program and your overall approach to coaching, rather than having them hear about it through the grapevine. You don't need to brief your team members on the actions you are taking with specific individuals on your team; individual coaching plans are private.

Aside from questions about the components of MOST, the question most likely asked by team members is when or if they will be coached using MOST. My recommendation is you ask each team member to think through the "define success" question that I discussed on page 92. When you sit down with them in a one-on-one session, you can discuss their answer to this question in context of their current performance and decide how they and the organization would benefit from a MOST coaching plan. Based upon these discussions, you can prioritize the rollout of MOST within your team.

You now have a framework to educate, build consensus and overcome any objections to the implementation of MOST in your organization.

<u>Key takeaways</u>

1. When implementing MOST, you do not change the existing _____ process.
2. You don't need more _____ to implement MOST.
3. MOST is a _____ coaching frame-work.

The answers are on page 135 and page 136.

Chapter Nine:

MOST™ REVIEW

The four phases of MOST™ and the key steps of each phase are as follows:

Phase 1: **Map**

> **Map** key skill gaps.
>
> Step 1: Determine and list the job's key skills and required proficiency level.
> Step 2: Determine and list the individual's key skills and proficiency level.
> Step 3: **Map** the two lists to determine an inventory of key skill gaps.

Phase 2: **Order**

> **Order** the resources that close key skill gaps.
>
> Step 1: Create a list of all potential resources.
> Step 2: Create a resource matrix for each skill gap.

Step 3: Prioritize the resources that best balance cost against impact.

Phase 3: **Structure**

Structure a coaching plan.

Step 1: Create a list of activities associated with each resource.
Step 2: List the expected outputs from performing any activity.
Step 3: Determine the impact on the key business metric.

Phase 4: **Track**

Track the results.

Step 1: Consolidate the outputs and impacts from the **Structure** phase.
Step 2: Assign start and end dates to each output and impact.
Step 3: Create a tracking template.

Chapter Ten:

MOST™ EXAMPLE

Throughout the book, I have used the MOST™ framework to create a coaching plan for George in his PM role. I will now use the MOST framework to create a coaching plan for Jennifer.

Jennifer was recently promoted into a sales manager position in her organization. The position involves prospecting for new clients, building relationships with existing clients, and meeting sales objectives. She does have some experience in sales and possesses a broad knowledge of the products and services sold by her organization, as she was the number one rated agent in her organization's inbound sales call center. Jennifer has strong communications skills and extensive experience as a negotiator partly because of an earlier job in the logistics department. She has limited experience prospecting for new clients and building relationships and sales with existing clients. Jennifer is a hard worker, considered a high potential employee and is highly motivated to succeed in her new position.

We'll work through all four phases of MOST to build a coaching plan for Jennifer.

<u>Jennifer</u>
<u>Sales Manager Role</u>

Phase 1: **Map**

Map the key skill gaps.

> Step 1: Determine and list the job's key skills and required proficiency level.
> Step 2: Determine and list the individual's key skills and proficiency level.
> Step 3: **Map** the two lists to determine an inventory of key skill gaps.

> Step 1: Determine and list the job's key skills and required proficiency level.

You will create the list of key skills associated with the job, and rate the proficiency required for each of these skills using a ten-point scale where one (1) is novice and ten (10) is expert. Remember, you're not rating the importance of each of the skills relative to each other. The job requires each of the skills you list. What you're doing is independently rating the required proficiency level for each skill.

After working through the activities described in Chapter Four, Jennifer created the following list of the required skills and their associated proficiency level needed to achieve success in her new role:

Job Required Key Skill	Rating (1–10)
Broad knowledge of products and services and associated benefits	10
Identify and develop new customer relationships	9
Build and maintain existing customer relationships	9
Experience in sales negotiation	8
Develop sales forecasts	8
Communications (written and verbal)	8

Step 2: Determine and list Jennifer's key skills and proficiency level.

Your discussions with Jennifer must focus on skills, not activities. These discussions yield the following list of her key skills and their associated level of proficiency:

Jennifer's Key Skill	Rating (1–10)
Broad knowledge of products and services and associated benefits	10
Experience in sales negotiations	9
Communications (written and verbal)	8
Identify and develop new customer relationships	3
Build and maintain existing customer relationships	3
Develop sales forecasts	3

Step 3: **Map** the two lists to determine an inventory of key skill gaps.

At this point, you have two lists; the list of skills and the associated proficiency level required to achieve job success and the list of skills and the associated proficiency level Jennifer possesses:

Key Skill	Rating (1–10)	
	Job Required	Jennifer
Broad knowledge of products and services and associated benefits	10	10
Identify and develop new customer relationships	9	3
Build and maintain existing customer relationships	9	3
Experience in sales negotiation	8	9
Develop sales forecasts	8	3
Communications (written and verbal)	8	8

By mapping these two lists, you can determine the skill proficiency gap (if any) between the skills required by the job and the skills possessed by Jennifer. You do this by subtracting the Job Required rating from the rating Jennifer gave herself for each skill. In the cases where Jennifer's skill rates less than the Job Required rating, you have a negative number that represents the size of the key skill gap. In cases where Jennifer's skill rates higher than the Job Required rating, you have a positive number that indicates you don't need to do any coaching in that area. In cases where Jennifer possesses a skill not needed for the job, she has an additional skill.

The output from mapping the two lists is as follows:

Job Required Key Skill	Proficiency Gap
Identify and develop new customer relationships	-6
Build and maintain existing customer relationships	-6
Develop sales forecasts	-5
Broad knowledge of products and services and associated benefits	0
Communications (written and verbal)	0
Experience in sales negotiation	+1

In summary, Jennifer will need to work on three key skills in the following order:

Job Required Key Skill	Proficiency Gap
Identify and develop new customer relationships	-6
Build and maintain existing customer relationships	-6
Develop sales forecasts	-5

Jennifer has the required level of expertise in two other key areas: her broad knowledge of products and services and communications. Jennifer also has a level of expertise in sales negotiation above that which the job requires.

Phase 2: **Order**

Order the resources that close key skill gaps.

Step 1: Create a list of all potential resources.
Step 2: Create a resource matrix for each skill gap.
Step 3: Prioritize the resources that best balance cost against impact.

Step 1: Create a list of all potential resources.

As you think through the resources at your disposal, I want to reiterate that Jennifer owns the plan. To that end, she needs to lead the efforts in thinking through prospective resources to assist her in closing the key skill gaps.

As you look to create a list of potential resources, you should note that a single resource may address multiple skill gaps, or you may need multiple resources to close a single skill gap. A sample of resources available to Jennifer includes, but is not limited to, the following:

1. Case studies
2. Role play
3. Professional trainer
4. Job shadowing
5. Internal training programs
6. External training programs
7. Special assignments
8. Volunteer work

In Chapter Five, I reviewed the above resources with the exception of case studies and role play. I will provide an overview of these two resources.

1.   Case studies

Case studies teach different lessons but when brainstorming with Jennifer, you are looking for company provided case studies that provide detail on the entire sales cycle including the company that purchased the products, the history of the sale, and how to calculate potential future sales. The studies should also have detailed information on the company policies and procedures for creating and updating the sales forecasts.

By working through a number of case studies, Jennifer can learn the practical aspects of creating and maintaining a sales forecast consistent with company policy and procedures.

2.   Role play

Role play takes many forms, but in this context, it refers to working with an experienced sales manager to simulate the interactions with customers through each step of the sales process; prospecting for new leads, making a sales pitch, overcoming objections, up-selling, closing the sale and account maintenance.

Step 2: Create a resource matrix for each skill gap.

Once you have come up with a list of all of the available resources, you need to create a matrix to classify each resource based upon its relative cost (X-axis) and its relative impact (Y-axis) on closing the skill gap. You need to create a resource matrix for each skill gap. By doing so, you can focus on the best way to close each specific skill gap.

Before we create the matrices, we must remember we are always looking to be a practical coach. Being practical means we strive to understand all of the costs and impacts associated with using a resource, but we don't need to spend hours determining the exact costs and impacts. We need to understand relative cost and impact.

The output from each matrix will assist you with Step 3 when you look to understand the relative value that each resource brings to closing the collective skill gaps and the overall cost/impact of each resource. Once we understand relative value, we can factor in our cost limitations to finalize our decision on what resource(s) to employ.

As you may recall from page 110, Jennifer needs to focus on closing the following key skill gaps:

Job Required Key Skill	Proficiency Gap
Identify and develop new customer relationships	-6
Build and maintain existing customer relationships	-6
Develop sales forecasts	-5

We will create a resource matrix for each of these key skill gaps.

<u>Identify and develop new customer relationships</u>

In the following matrix (Figure 6), I classify each resource based upon its relative cost (X-axis) and impact (Y-axis) on closing the skill gap associated with identifying and developing new customer relationships.

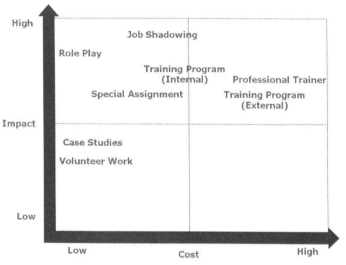

Figure 6: Resource matrix for identifying and developing new customer relationships

The focus on creating this matrix is to ensure Jennifer has the opportunity to interact with other sales managers and, by doing so, gain the experience and feedback necessary to identify and develop new customer relationships.

Job shadowing is the most efficient and effective way for Jennifer to achieve this goal, especially if afforded the opportunity to job shadow full-time. Full-time job shadowing means she works closely with the selected sales manager on every aspect of the job throughout the designated period. In cases of full-time job shadowing, you need to determine how much time is sufficient for Jennifer to experience all aspects of the sale cycle, albeit with different customers. For ease of discussion, we will assume a full-time job shadow assignment will last six weeks.

Role-playing is an efficient and effective option, especially when paired with job shadowing.

An internal training program can provide cost/impact benefit but training courses related to sales often lack the opportunity to practice the dynamic customer facing skills that are part of the sales environment.

A professional trainer has an impact on this key skill gap but he or she may not have experience specific to the organization and is more expensive than other options.

External training programs can be less effective than other options given they may not focus on the specific business issues important to Jennifer and they can be more costly than internal training programs.

A special assignment would be helpful if focused in the sales area.

Case studies are a less dynamic way to learn the required skills but may provide some assistance in learning how the company approaches and wins business.

Depending on the nature of the work, time spent volunteering can provide the opportunity to practice these sales skills.

At this point, we have completed a matrix for the skill gap associated with identifying and developing new customer relationships and have determined that full-time job shadowing coupled with role-play during the job shadowing period provide the best cost/impact options to close this specific skill gap.

Build and maintain existing customer relationships

In the following matrix (Figure 7), I classify each resource based upon its relative cost (X-axis) and impact (Y-axis) on closing the key skill gap associated with building and maintaining existing customer relationships.

Figure 7: Resource matrix for building and maintaining existing customer relationships

The focus on creating this matrix is to ensure that Jennifer has the opportunity to interact with other sales managers and, by doing so, gain the experience and feedback necessary to learn how her company builds and maintains existing customer relationships.

Given the similarity with the focus of the first matrix, a practical approach dictates that we select the same set of resources; full-time job shadowing coupled with role-play to close this specific skill gap.

Develop sales forecasts

In the following matrix (Figure 8), I classify each resource based upon its relative cost (X-axis) and impact (Y-axis) on closing the key skill gap associated with developing sales forecasts.

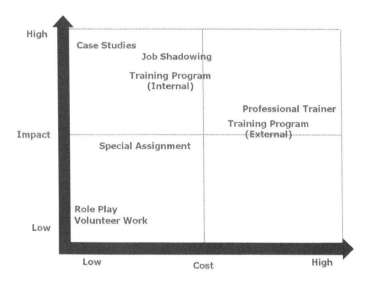

Figure 8: Resource matrix for developing sales forecasts

The focus on creating this matrix is to ensure Jennifer learns how to develop sales forecasts in accordance with company policy and procedures.

Using case studies is the most efficient and effective way to achieve this goal, especially if afforded the opportunity to work through the case studies while job shadowing.

An internal training program is effective but may not provide the same level of hands-on experience associated with job shadowing.

A professional trainer, external training programs, role-play or special assignment are either too costly or less efficient when compared with the opportunity for Jennifer to review actual case study data under the tutelage of the manager associated with her job shadowing.

Volunteer work does not provide the opportunity to practice the required skills.

At this point, we have completed a matrix for the skill gap associated with developing sales forecasts and have determined that using case studies provides the best cost/impact option to close this specific skill gap.

Step 3: Prioritize the resources that best balance cost against impact.

In this step, you take the prioritized list of key skill gaps and the output from the resource matrices to determine which resources provide you the best collective cost/impact to close your skill gaps.

Cost/impact balance is important to the integrity of MOST. You want to select only those resources with the greatest impact on the key skill gaps that Jennifer needs to close for the least cost. Least cost doesn't mean little or no cost. In some cases, the most expensive resource is essential, and though expensive, it may be the least costly as it is the only resource that impacts the skill gap you want to close.

Additionally, an expensive resource that assists in closing all of the known skill gaps may provide more cost/impact than a single cheaper resource that closes only one skill gap. Lastly, you may find that you do not have to utilize all or even most of the resources that you came up with in Step 1 if a single resource can meet all of your needs.

We can now examine the skill gaps we need to close and the collective results from the resource matrices:

Job Required Key Skill	Proficiency Gap	Resource Matrix Results
Identify and develop new customer relationships	-6	Job shadowing and role play
Build and maintain existing customer relationships	-6	Job shadowing and role play
Develop sales forecasts	-5	Case studies

In summary, when we consider that job shadowing and role-play close the two highest priority skill gaps and case studies are the best resource to close the sales forecasting skill gap, the practical decision is to focus Jennifer's coaching plan in three areas:

1. A full-time job shadow opportunity with a seasoned sales manager
2. Role-playing
3. Working through case studies

You may recall from our example with George that I advocated using only two resources for his coaching plan (internal training program and job shadowing) and not three resources (internal training program, job shadowing, and special assignment). In his case, the rationale was that the internal training program and job shadowing address all of the skill gaps with a focus on the most important skill gap, PM software proficiency. Therefore, the practical decision was to use only two resources.

With Jennifer, the practical decision is to employ three resources; job shadowing, role playing, and case studies. These resources dovetail together with minimal additional time, money, or effort needed to incorporate a third resource, case studies, into Jennifer's coaching plan.

Phase 3: **Structure**

Structure a coaching plan.

Step 1: Create a list of activities associated with each resource.

Step 2: List the expected outputs from performing any activity.

Step 3: Determine the impact on the key business metric.

As you may recall from the **Map** and **Order** phases, we learned about Jennifer and her skill gaps and the resources available to close those skill gaps. We determined we were going to focus Jennifer's coaching plan on three resources: job shadowing, role-playing, and case studies.

Job Required Key Skill	Proficiency Gap	Resource Matrix Results
Identify and develop new customer relationships	-6	Job shadowing and role play
Build and maintain existing customer relationships	-6	Job shadowing and role play
Develop sales forecasts	-5	Case studies

Job shadowing

Job Required Key Skill	Proficiency Gap	Resource Matrix Results
Identify and develop new customer relationships	-6	Job shadowing
Build and maintain existing customer relationships	-6	Job shadowing

Step 1: Create a list of activities associated with each resource.

1. Select and introduce a sales manager for a six-week job shadow period
2. Attend sales calls with existing and potential customers
3. Perform follow-up activities associated with sales calls
4. Attend team meetings and planning sessions to identify potential sales leads
5. Review sales forecasts

Step 2: List the expected outputs from performing any activity.

1. Start and finish dates for job shadow activities
2. Bi-weekly one-page report on lessons learned with a focus on the specific actions that will be taken to do the following:
    a. Identify and contact potential customers
    b. Deepen relationships and increase sales with existing clients
3. Bi-weekly feedback from the Sales Manager Jennifer is shadowing:
    a. Structured checklist with specific feedback on Jennifer's performance that covers the following:
        i.   Ability to identify sales leads
        ii. Ability to determine appropriate product sets to pitch to new customers
        iii. Ability to up-sell existing customers based upon customer needs
        iv. Input at sales planning meetings

Step 3: Determine the impact on the key business metric.

1. Identify, contact, and add new customers to client list: 10% increase in new customer acquisitions within six months of having her own accounts.

2.   Spend by existing customers: 5% increase within six months of having her own accounts.

Determining the impact of any activity on a key metric can be difficult. However, you can determine a reasonable expectation for improvement based upon business objectives. In this case, Jennifer and her coach have agreed that once she is assigned her own accounts, she should be able to grow the client list 10% and drive a 5% increase in spend from existing customers over the first six months. Progress towards these goals will be measured each month.

<u>Role-playing</u>

Job Required Key Skill	Proficiency Gap	Resource Matrix Results
Identify and develop new customer relationships	-6	Role play
Build and maintain existing customer relationships	-6	Role play

Step 1: Create a list of activities associated with each resource.

1. Select and introduce sales manager (same manager as for job shadowing)
2. Conduct role-play exercises weekly. Specific scenarios include, but are not limited to the following:
    a. Prospecting for new leads
    b. Making a sales pitch
    c. Overcoming objections
    d. Up-selling to existing customers
    e. Closing the sale

Step 2: List the expected outputs from performing any activity.

1. Start and finish dates for role-play activities
2. Bi-weekly feedback from the Sales Manager Jennifer is shadowing:
    a. Structured checklist with specific feedback on Jennifer's performance during role play scenarios

Step 3: Determine the impact on the key business metric.

1. Identify, contact, and add new customers to client list: 10% increase in new customer acquisitions within six months of having her own accounts.

2.   Spend by existing customers: 5% increase within six months of having her own accounts.

Jennifer and her coach have earlier agreed that a 10% increase in the number of new customers and 5% increase in spending by existing customers reflect the impact of job shadowing. Role play complements the job shadowing and impacts the same key metrics. Given the complementary nature of these two resources, we will consider the impact on the key metrics is a collective 10% increase in the number of new customers and a 5% increase in spending by existing customers within six months of Jennifer having her own accounts.

Case studies

Job Required Key Skill	Proficiency Gap	Resource Matrix Results
Develop sales forecasts	-5	Case studies

Step 1: Create a list of activities associated with each resource.

1.   Select and review case studies

Step 2: List the expected outputs from performing any activity.

1. Work through case studies during job shadow period
2. Detailed sales forecasts for three accounts produced after four weeks of job shadowing

Step 3: Determine the impact on the key business metric.

1. Monthly sales forecast created; accurate within company guidelines

By working through the case studies, Jennifer will create and maintain her sales forecasts within the company guidelines.

In summary, the impact of applying all three resources to close Jennifer's skill gaps is a 10% increase in new customers and 5% increase in spending by existing customers within six months of Jennifer having her own accounts. Jennifer will also be able to produce sales forecasts accurate within the company guidelines.

Phase 4: **Track**

Track the results.

Step 1: Consolidate the outputs and impacts from the **Structure** phase.

Step 2: Assign start and end dates to each output and impact.
Step 3: Create a tracking template.

Step 1: Consolidate the outputs and impacts from the **Structure** phase.

We know from the **Structure** phase that we are going to utilize three resources in Jennifer's coaching plan: job shadowing, role-play, and case studies. As we consolidate all the outputs and impacts and eliminate duplicated items, we have a finalized list of what we need to track.

Consolidated outputs

1. Start and finish dates for job shadowing activities
2. Start and finish dates for role-play activities
3. Work through case studies during job shadow period
4. Bi-weekly, one-page report on lessons learned
5. Bi-weekly feedback from the Sales Manager Jennifer is shadowing
6. Detailed sales forecasts for three accounts produced after four weeks of job shadowing

Consolidated impacts

1. Identify, contact, and add new customers to client list: 10% increase in new customer acquisitions within six months of having her own accounts.
2. Spend by existing customers: 5% increase within six months of having her own accounts.
3. Monthly sales forecast created; accurate within company guidelines

Step 2: Assign start and end dates to each output and impact.

As we look to assign start and end dates, we know that job shadowing, role-playing, and the review of case studies all start on Day One and last six weeks. We will assume Jennifer is assigned her own accounts the day after completion of the job shadow assignment. Over the first six months, she needs to generate a 10% increase in the number of her accounts and a 5% increase in revenue for her accounts, and she needs to create and maintain her sales forecasts within company guidelines.

Using the above assumptions, we get the following dates for Jennifer's coaching plan:

1. Start and end date of job shadowing, role-playing, and case study review: Day 1 to Day 40

2. Start date of bi-weekly lessons learned and feedback report from Sales Manager: Day 12 recurring every ten business days

3. Due date for sales forecasts for three accounts: Day 29

4. End date of bi-weekly lessons learned and feedback report: Day 40

5. Start managing own accounts: Day 43

6. Monthly status report including sales forecasts, number of accounts and revenue increase of assigned accounts: Day 66 and last day of each month thereafter

Step 3: Create a tracking template.

We will enter all start and end dates into a project management template. I will illustrate the tracking template entries for outputs and impacts for the first 100 days:

Day	Entry
1	Start of job shadowing, role-play, and case study review
12	Start date of bi-weekly lessons learned and feedback report
26	Bi-weekly lessons learned and feedback report
29	Jennifer presents sales forecasts for three accounts
40	End of job shadowing. Last bi-weekly lessons learned and feedback report

43	Jennifer assigned her own accounts
66	Monthly status report including sales forecasts, number of accounts, and revenue increase of assigned accounts
97	Monthly status report including sales forecasts, number of accounts, and revenue increase of assigned accounts

Congratulations. You and Jennifer have completed all four phases of MOST. You now have a practical and structured coaching plan focused on the improvement of key skills that impact results, and you have a tracking template to ensure you stay focused on your plan.

Chapter Eleven:

KEY TAKEAWAYS

I want to provide a summary of the key takeaways from each chapter as a ready reference.

Chapter One: What is coaching?

1. Coaching is a series of <u>interactions</u> between individuals focused on the <u>identification</u> and subsequent <u>improvement</u> of a key skill needed to achieve an <u>agreed-upon</u> goal.
2. Coaching is often confused with other activities such as <u>training</u>, <u>mentoring</u>, and <u>managing</u>.
3. The MOST coaching framework simplifies the coaching process into <u>four</u> phases.

Chapter Two: Why Coach?

1. A coaching culture directly and positively affects the organization's <u>bottom</u> line.
2. MOST is a <u>repeatable</u> process.

ANTHONY CONNOLLY

3.   Using MOST leads to the following:
      a.   Achievement of <u>performance</u> goals
      b.   Improvement of organizational <u>efficiency</u>
      c.   Improvement of business <u>acumen</u>
      d.   <u>Reputation</u> building
      e.   Sense of <u>accomplishment</u>

Chapter Three: Guiding Principles

1.   <u>Be respectful</u>: Frame the coaching relation-
      ship as just that - a relationship.
2.   <u>Set goals</u>: Coach to a definable and measur-
      able goal or set of goals.
3.   <u>Take ownership</u>: The person you are coaching
      owns the coaching plan.

Chapter Four: **Map**

1.   You must differentiate skill from <u>activity</u>.
2.   <u>Independently</u> rate the proficiency of each re-
      quired job skill.
3.   The **Map** phase has three steps:
      a.   Determine and list the <u>job's</u> key skills
            and <u>required</u> proficiency level.
      b.   Determine and list the <u>individual's</u> key
            skills and proficiency level.
      c.   **Map** the two lists to determine an <u>inven-
            tory</u> of key skill gaps.

Chapter Five: **Order**

1. <u>Cost/Impact</u> is a key theme in the **Order** phase of MOST.
2. You need to be able to <u>measure</u> the impact of any resource you employ.
3. Least cost doesn't mean <u>little or no cost</u>.

Chapter Six: **Structure**

1. <u>Set goals</u>: Is the key guiding principle of the **Structure** phase of MOST.
2. You need to bridge <u>activities</u> to <u>outputs</u> and <u>outputs</u> to <u>impacts</u>.
3. You use a <u>common-sense</u> approach to determine the impact on key metrics.

Chapter Seven: **Track**

1. Eliminate <u>duplicate</u> items when you consolidate outputs and impacts.
2. Coaching is not a <u>one-time</u> event.
3. Tracking templates don't need to be <u>complicated</u>.

Chapter Eight: Implementing MOST

1. When implementing MOST, you do not change the existing <u>evaluation</u> process.

2. You don't need more <u>money</u> to implement MOST.

3. MOST is a <u>collaborative</u> coaching framework.

COACHING IN THE REAL WORLD

Throughout this book, I have focused on using MOST™ to ensure that you spend your time and effort only on those coaching activities that drive results. In keeping with this practical approach, we'll solve Laura's coaching issues by moving from her "fire" approach to the MOST coaching framework.

Let's begin with a quick summary of her situation:

- Laura is concerned about her team making her revenue objective.
- She has two low performers: Jack and Francis.
- She has two strong performers.
- She has five solid performers.
- She has two new team members carrying a 50% revenue objective: Harvey and Tracey.

Laura will first need to educate, build consensus, and overcome any objections with her key stakeholders before implementing MOST.

As a first step, she'll get buy-in from her boss Allison to implement MOST. We'll assume Allison is supportive of any approach that keeps the existing evaluation process, doesn't need additional funding, and will assist Laura in meeting her revenue objective.

Laura then has to decide upon the best candidates for the initial rollout of MOST. Given her concern about making her revenue objective, she has four potential candidates: Jack, Francis, Harvey, and Tracey. Given the potential shown by Harvey, the experience Tracey brings to the job, and that they are carrying a 50% revenue objective for the next two months, Laura does not consider them the number one priority. Laura will focus her coaching efforts on Jack and Francis.

Laura will discuss MOST with them, in separate one-on-one meetings. She'll overcome any objections they may have and work with each of them to create a specific coaching plan using MOST. She will also brief her team members on the MOST coaching framework so everyone understands her new approach to coaching.

Once she has a MOST program up and running for Jack and Francis, she can monitor their progress against their plan using her tracking sheet. She can determine, based upon her team results and one-on-one discussions with the rest of her team members, if she needs to roll out MOST to any other team members and, if so, in what priority.

Laura is free of the "fire" approach to coaching. By implementing MOST, Laura is able to focus her coaching efforts on selected individuals and improve their key skills that directly impact the attainment of their revenue objective and, by extension, her revenue objective.

FINAL THOUGHTS

<u>I believe in you</u>

I have created a practical approach to coaching that recognizes and reflects the reality that you have a limited amount of time to coach. I have done so because without you, there is no coaching.

<u>I believe in results</u>

Coaching is an investment and like any investment, it requires a return. In the case of coaching, the required return is consistently better results.

<u>I believe in MOST™</u>

The MOST coaching framework provides the practical approach you need to focus your coaching efforts in the areas that drive consistently better results.

ACKNOWLEDGEMENTS

Writing this book would only have been possible with the feedback, support, and encouragement of a great number of people. In particular, I would like to thank the following individuals:

Mr. Walter Anderson, Vice-President of Operations for Anderson Recruiting (www.andersonrecruiting.com). His insight and advice sharpened the focus of the book and his friendship kept me motivated to finish.

Mr. Michael Bishop, General Counsel for AT&T Intellectual Property, Inc. His probing questions and comments brought clarity to my writing.

Mrs. Christine Igot, Professor of French at Université Sainte-Anne, Nova Scotia, Canada. Her experience teaching thousands of students assisted in creating a more readable version of the book.

Mrs. P. Jane Nicholson of Mrs. Nicholson Home (www.mrsnicholsonhome.com). Her support was unflagging, her feedback insightful, and her punctuation, as always, perfect.

Mr. David Taylor, Partner with Pantelis, Inc. (www.pantelis-inc.com). As a retired Army officer and leadership change consultant, David asked me the difficult questions regarding the implementation of the MOST™ coaching framework.

Ms. Tara Dawn Williams. Her love and support is a never-ending source of encouragement to me.

ABOUT THE AUTHOR

Anthony has spent more than 25 years working with and coaching individuals and teams. His experiences include serving as an Engineering Officer in the Royal Canadian Navy, collaborating with and leading unionized and contractor workforces and holding numerous operational and sales leadership positions within Fortune 25 companies. Anthony participates in and leads volunteer efforts with for-profit and not-for profit institutions and for the past eight years has provided team and individual level coaching to executive MBA students enrolled in the Coles College of Business at Kennesaw State University.

Anthony received a B.Sc. in Applied Sciences from the Royal Military College of Canada in 1987 and an M.B.A. from the Coles College of Business at Kennesaw State University in 1999. He earned a certificate in Managerial Coaching from Kennesaw State University in 2009.

Anthony and his wife, Tara, reside in Roswell, GA. He can be reached through his website; www.AppliedCoachingSolutions.com or directly at Anthony@AppliedCoachingSolutions.com

NOTES

33198652R00094

Made in the USA
Charleston, SC
06 September 2014